MW00936368

Norway Travel Guide 2024

Norway throughout the year: The perfect trip to Norway

Table of Contents

Chapter 1. Introduction to Norway

Welcome to Norway

As you begin your journey to Norway, you are about to discover a world of stunning landscapes, a rich cultural past, and lovely people. A region where ancient history and cutting-edge technology coexist, beautiful mountains guard serene fjords, and the midnight sun and the Northern Lights paint the sky with mesmerising colours, this Scandinavian gem is a place where you may experience all of these things.

Your adventure starts in the vibrant capital city of Oslo, which is snuggled away between the Oslofjord and lush hills. Learn about the magnificent blend of old and modern architecture, from the Middle Ages' Akershus Fortress to the wonderfully futuristic Opera House. Discover Vigeland Park, a celebration of connection and passion between people, where more than 200 of Gustav Vigeland's sculptures have come to life.

As you travel west, you will come across the UNESCO-listed fjords, which were created by ancient glaciers. Whether you are sailing through Geirangerfjord, with its breathtaking waterfalls cascading down high cliffs, or discovering Naeroyfjord, the smallest fjord in the world, you will be in awe of the sheer majesty of these natural wonders.

For the daring, Norway offers a broad range of thrilling outdoor activities. You'll feel almost surreal as you drive down the well-known Trolltunga road because of the breathtaking views. Skiers' paradises include winter wonderlands like Trysil and Hemsedal, where pristine slopes and cosy lodges are waiting.

Another is the beauty of the Northern Lights. The polar sky is coloured with dancing lights, which also brighten the night with colour. Come to Troms, sometimes known as the "Gateway to the Arctic," to see this celestial spectacle up close. You'll always have this memory with you.

Remember to familiarise yourself with Norway's diverse traditions and culture. Try some of the age-old customary dishes, such rakfisk (fermented fish) and frikl (stew of lamb and cabbage). Explore Bergen's historic Hanseatic waterfront, which has pleasant cafés and unique shops housed in vibrant wooden buildings.

Explore the colourful local culture by going to the Sámi areas in the north. Visit reindeer herding settlements to learn about their rituals and learn about the significance of the lavvu tents that dot the landscape.

As you go through this breathtaking area, you will come to understand the genuine warmth and compassion of the Norwegian people. Their profound love of nature and the outdoors will make you feel at home even in a foreign land, as will their genuine welcome.

Bring your sense of wonder since Norway has a way of leaving you in awe at every turn. Take photos of the magnificent fjords, inhale the clean mountain air, and let the tranquillity of the surroundings uplift your soul.

Whether you decide to embark on an adventurous adventure, take a leisurely stroll through lovely cities, or sip hot chocolate by a roaring fire, Norway promises to be an experience unlike any other. It's a place where it seems like time has stood still, allowing you to fully appreciate the moment and create lifetime memories.

Therefore, as soon as you set foot on Norwegian soil, let the journey of discovery and astonishment begin, my fellow traveller. As you open your heart to the magic that awaits, let Norway's beauty fascinate you in ways you never thought possible. I hope your stay here is joyful, exciting, and full of the types of experiences you'll always love. Hello from Norway!

Geography and Climate

Norway is a fascinating location for tourists seeking a variety of natural beauty and outdoor adventures because of its captivating terrain and unique climate. The northern European nation of Norway is home to serene lakes, lush forests, gorgeous mountains, and impressive fjords. Explorers and environmental enthusiasts may choose from a variety of activities thanks to its geographic features.

Norway's fjords are without a doubt its most identifiable geographical feature. These ancient glaciers carved out these deep, narrow inlets, which are surrounded by steep cliffs and rough mountain ranges. The Geirangerfjord and the Naeroyfjord are two UNESCO World Heritage Sites that provide excellent examples of this stunning natural phenomenon. To see the beauty of these settings up close, tourists may join fjord cruises, often passing picturesque settlements perched along the coastline and cascading waterfalls.

In addition to its fjords, Norway is known for its rough terrain. The Scandinavian Mountains, which make up a significant chunk of the country's western border, provide wonderful opportunities for climbing, skiing, and hiking. One of Norway's highest peaks, Galdhpiggen, is situated in Jotunheimen National Park. Hikers may go on well marked trails that wind through lush valleys, alpine meadows, and glacier-carved landscapes, providing breathtaking panoramic views at every turn.

Along Norway's expansive coastline, the North Sea and Norwegian Sea are studded with many islands. Coastal towns like Bergen and Lesund, which are magnificent combinations of bustling ports, colourful wooden buildings, and thriving fish markets, provide a view into the country's maritime heritage. The Lofoten Islands, with their towering peaks and charming fishing villages, are a photographer's paradise and a terrific site to see the midnight sun in the summer.

The country's latitude and the North Atlantic Drift, a minor ocean current that moderates temperatures along the shore, have a considerable influence on the climate. Norway has a milder climate than one would expect given its latitude. In the summer, temperatures often vary from 15°C to 25°C (59°F to 77°F), which is a pleasant range, especially near the seaside. There are many outdoor activities and exploration options at this time of year.

Norway's climate may be somewhat erratic, even in the summer. Rainfall is common, particularly close to the western shore where the mountains redirect moist air masses from the ocean, creating lush vegetation and lovely waterfalls. Travellers should pack enough layers of clothing and be prepared for sudden weather changes.

The winter season in Norway offers an experience that is totally different but no less spectacular. The country's northern regions, such Tromso and Alta, are good locations to see the mesmerising Northern Lights. From October through March, the Arctic night sky is alive with dazzling displays of green, pink, and purple lights.

Due to its stunning environment, Norway is a haven for fans of winter sports. Numerous well-maintained ski resorts around the country provide slopes for skiers of all abilities and offer popular winter activities like skiing and snowboarding. Cross-country skiing is ingrained in Norwegian culture, and the nation has a wide network of trails that wind through forests, mountains, and even urban areas.

In conclusion, the geography and climate of Norway provide for a wide range of exciting experiences for visitors. Norway's natural wonders, which include spectacular fjords, mountains, charming coastal communities, and the Northern Lights, will astound anybody who comes. Norway is a destination that, whether you're an adventurer, a nature lover, or simply want to immerse yourself in the beauty of the outdoors, will provide lifetime memories and a connection with nature's most beautiful creations.

Chapter 2. Planning Your Trip

Best Time to Visit

Norway's breathtaking landscapes, magnificent fjords, and vibrant cities make it a year-round traveller's paradise. However, how you feel about this Nordic wonder depends much on the season you visit. Because of its unique mix of cultural events, outdoor activities, and natural phenomena, the best time to visit Norway depends on your interests and tastes.

Summer (June–August): Without a doubt, summer is the most favoured time of year to go to Norway due to the wonderful weather and fascinating events. With temperatures typically ranging from 60 to 70 degrees Fahrenheit (15 to 25 degrees Celsius), the summertime provides a tranquil environment for outdoor exploration. The days are very long, and northern regions like Troms—where the sun never completely sets—experience the Midnight Sun phenomena.

Summer is the ideal season for individuals who like hiking, biking, and exploring the famous fjords. It is a photographer's dream since the vivid colours bring the lush surroundings to life. In the bustling coastal towns and cities, there are a plethora of festivals celebrating music, art, and local culture.

Autumn (September to October): As the summer crowds start to disperse, Norway becomes quieter and more tranquil. The landscapes take on a tapestry of warm and golden tones even as the temperatures begin to fall. For those who like more solitude while still being able to go hiking and fishing outdoors, this is a terrific time. The Northern Lights also start to appear in the latter nights, adding a sense of awe to your journey.

Winter (November to February): One of nature's most captivating displays, the Northern Lights, are a well-known feature of Norway's winters. As the country changes into a snowy wonderland, a range of winter sports are offered, including dog sledding, skiing, and snowboarding as well as ice fishing. The ability to warm oneself in front of a fire and the charming ambience of the towns make up for the fact that it may be extremely chilly, especially in the north.

The Christmas markets and other festive events make winter a particularly delightful season. You could even have the chance to see the Polar Night in the far north, when the sun doesn't rise over the horizon for many weeks.

Spring (March–May): Spring in Norway is a season of regeneration and awakening as the temperatures begin to rise and the snow begins to melt. Skiers who are serious about their sport say that right now is the best time to enjoy the snow that is still on the ground and observe the transition from winter to summer. Despite the cold temperatures in March and April, the flowers and greenery are back by May, creating stunning vistas.

The spring is a good time to go since it is less crowded and there are less tourists around. May is National Day in Norway, which is celebrated with parades, traditional dress, and a strong sense of nationalism.

In conclusion, the best time to visit Norway will mostly rely on your interests and the things you want to see and do there. Each season offers a unique attraction and a range of activities, from the Midnight Sun and outdoor excursions in the summer to the ethereal magnificence of the Northern Lights in the winter. Whether you're a nature lover, a culture vulture, or simply searching for a nice hideaway, Norway has a lot to offer all year long.

Entry Requirements

Beautiful fjords, picturesque landscapes, and a vibrant cultural past will all be there for those who are thinking about taking a trip to Norway. Before setting off on their journey, it's crucial to be aware of the requirements for entering the country. Thanks to these requirements, travellers will have an easy and hassle-free experience, allowing them to fully enjoy everything Norway has to offer.

A visa is often the first entry requirement that comes to mind for travellers. Norway, however, is a party to the Schengen Agreement, which permits travellers from certain countries to enter visa-free for short stays. The people of the European Union (EU) and the countries that make up the European Free Trade Association (EFTA), such as Switzerland, Iceland, and Liechtenstein, are affected by this. Furthermore, visitors from a number of other countries, such as the United States, Canada, Australia, and Japan, do not need a visa in order to stay in Norway for up to 90 days during the course of 180 days. Before leaving, make sure you have the most up-to-date information since visa requirements might sometimes change.

While certain travellers may not need a visa, everyone must have a current passport. When leaving the Schengen Zone, your passport must still be valid at least three months later. If travellers' travel plans are changed or delayed, this legislation shields them against unpleasant shocks.

A crucial element of the entry requirements is travel insurance. Even though Norway boasts a top-notch healthcare system, visitors may nevertheless have to pay high medical expenses. It is strongly encouraged to get travel insurance that covers medical situations in order to have peace of mind when travelling. In the case of illness or accidents, having enough insurance may shield travellers from unanticipated financial difficulties.

When visiting Norway, it's also essential to have proof of your housing and enough cash on hand to cover your stay's expenditures. This may be shown by hotel reservations, an invitation from a host, or other documented evidence of the living arrangements. It is customary to request evidence of financial stability to ensure that visitors won't put an excessive burden on the host country's resources.

Customs rules are yet another essential element of the admittance requirements. Norway has strict regulations on what may be brought in. Weapons, narcotics, and a few types of food are all forbidden things. Travellers should familiarise themselves with the necessary procedures in order to avoid any legal implications upon arrival.

It's important to note that depending on whether a person enters by land, sea, or air, admission requirements and border formalities could change. When going by air, be prepared for the standard passport checks, security checks, and customs inspections. Passengers entering via border crossings on foot or by boat may be subject to similar examinations.

To guarantee a quick entrance process, travellers should get the necessary papers well in advance and confirm that they meet the requirements. It's important to stay current with travel advisories and entry criteria, especially in the fast-changing world we live in today.

In conclusion, Norway's entry requirements are designed to ensure the ease, safety, and comfort of both visitors and the host country. Being well-prepared, which includes possessing a current passport, travel insurance, and complying with customs rules, ensures a pleasant and trouble-free vacation to this stunning Scandinavian area.

Transportation

There are many different modes of transportation available for tourists who want to experience Norway's magnificent landscapes, charming towns, and cultural attractions. Travel choices in Norway range from gorgeous road trips to efficient public transit systems.

For travellers arriving by air, the biggest airports in Norway, such as Oslo Gardermoen, Bergen

Flesland, and Trondheim Vaernes, provide easy entrance points. Passengers may easily travel to Norway from many different areas across the world because of these airports' good connections to a broad variety of international locales. Once in Norway, tourists may simply go on to the next leg of their journey.

Using Norway's extensive rail system is one of the most popular and efficient ways to travel around the nation. Operated by the Norwegian State Railways (NSB), the Oslo to Bergen "Bergen Line" passes through stunning fjords, harsh terrain, and attractive villages. The "Flm Railway," which offers a quick but beautiful ride through some of the country's most magnificent views, is another destination.

For individuals who want their travels to be independent, renting a car is a terrific option. Norway's well-kept highways wind through gorgeous countryside, making for an enjoyable drive. The "Atlantic Road" is a must-drive route that provides amazing ocean views as it seems to float over the water. Driving in Norway, however, requires adhering to strict traffic laws and being considerate of animal crossings.

Considering Norway's extensive coastline and many islands, ferries are essential for getting around. Visitors may get a unique picture of Norway's coastline beauty on ferry rides. On a Hurtigruten cruise along the Norwegian coast, tourists may see the captivating Northern Lights in the winter or the Midnight Sun in the summer.

For travellers that care about the environment, Norway boasts a fantastic public transportation system that includes buses, trams, and boats. Major cities like Oslo, Bergen, and Trondheim, which have well-developed networks, make it possible to visit metropolitan areas without a car. The introduction of electric buses and trams in Norway demonstrates the country's commitment to sustainability and reducing its carbon impact.

Cyclists may traverse Norway's stunning landscapes by bicycle. The country features a huge network of bicycle lanes, with options for skilled riders as well as leisurely rides through quaint villages and challenging mountain climbs. Given that many locations provide bike rental services, tourists may embark on riding excursions.

Travellers may combine several modes of transportation to create unique itineraries. For instance, a journey can include taking the train to a remote place and then renting a car to explore unexplored areas. The excitement of the voyage is increased by the use of so many different forms of transportation.

It's crucial to remember that Norway's transportation system has a reputation for dependability and punctuality. Weather, however, may sometimes affect schedules, especially in remote areas or during the winter. Before leaving on a vacation, be sure to confirm the most latest information.

In conclusion, Norway's tourist transit system seamlessly blends modern efficiency with untouched beauty. Norway provides a smooth and enjoyable way to explore its many landscapes and immerse oneself in its vibrant culture, from breathtaking road trips and breathtaking train journeys to environmentally friendly urban transportation options.

Chapter 3. Top Destinations

Oslo

Due to its location in one of Norway's most beautiful natural settings, Oslo, the capital city, stands out as a top option for travellers seeking a diverse array of cultural, historical, and natural experiences. Oslo's seamless combination of traditional beauty and modern innovation offers tourists an exciting experience that immerses them in the spirit of Norway's past and present.

One of Oslo's most notable features is its deep historical heritage, which is reflected in its architecture and monuments. The Akershus fortification is an illustration of a mediaeval fortification that proudly overlooks the Oslofjord and offers a view into Norway's vibrant past. After being built to protect the city in the beginning, the stronghold has seen centuries of history and now serves as a living museum, hosting events, exhibitions, and guided tours.

Due to its commanding elevation that provides panoramic views of the city and the fjord, it is a must-visit place for history aficionados and visitors alike.

Royal Majesty: The Royal Palace, a magnificent example of neoclassicism, serves as the official residence of the Norwegian king. The palace is a reminder of the nation's imperial heritage. It is surrounded by lush gardens and has a peaceful atmosphere. Visitors are welcome to see the daily tradition of the Changing of the Guard, which adds a touch of royal grandeur to the splendour of the city. The palace is sometimes open to the public so that they may see the opulent interiors and learn more about Norway's royal family.

A rich tapestry of galleries, museums, and creative possibilities make up Oslo's cultural scene. Huge Vigeland Park, named for famous artist Gustav Vigeland, is a sanctuary of art and environment. The more than 200 sculptures in the park, which is composed of wrought iron, granite, and bronze, portray many aspects of the human experience. Information about Vigeland's life and creative process is available at the neighbouring Vigeland Museum.

Oslo is a haven for those who appreciate the arts. The Munch Museum celebrates Edvard Munch, the most well-known artist from Norway, by showcasing his well-known painting "The Scream" along with a variety of his other works. A substantial collection of Norwegian and international artwork, including works by well-known painters like Carl Larsson and Johan Christian Dahl, can be found at the National Gallery. On the other side, the Astrup Fearnley Museum offers contemporary art in a stunning waterfront setting and offers a modern perspective.

Given Oslo's proximity to the Oslofjord, maritime experiences are a major draw for visitors. Travellers may benefit from boat excursions that provide vast views of the city's coastline and assist them in comprehending how urban development and the surrounding natural beauty coexist. The Oslo Opera House, an architectural wonder that seems to rise from the fjord, is a must-see. Because of its contemporary construction, which offers a distinctive vantage point for both the city and the lake, visitors are urged to explore on its sloping top.

Delicious Food: Oslo's culinary scene has evolved into a fusion of tradition and innovation. In the gourmet haven known as the Mathallen Food Hall, local manufacturers sell their handmade cheeses, cured meats, chocolates, and seafood. The hall exemplifies Norway's commitment to ecological and organic cuisine by allowing visitors to experience true flavours while supporting local companies. Visitors seeking a fine-dining experience may see Norway's culinary skill at Maaemo, a restaurant with three Michelin stars.

Oslo's embracing of the outdoors will reassure those who value nature. The enormous Oslomarka forest, which surrounds the city, has a variety of hiking and skiing trails. The serene lakes and warm cottages provide a break from the bustle of city life. The Holmenkollen Ski Jump, a well-known landmark, not only hosts ski competitions but also offers thrill-seeking experiences to visitors anxious to descend the ski jump.

Year-Round Magic: Oslo's appeal remains constant despite the ebbs and flows of the seasons. With outdoor festivals, concerts, and celebrations of music, the arts, and culture, the city comes to life in the summer. Both residents and tourists make the most of the additional daylight hours by going to parks and doing outdoor activities. Oslo transforms into a stunning wonderland in the winter when it is completely blanketed in snow, inviting visitors to enjoy ice skating, winter sports, and the cosy warmth of cafés and restaurants.

Oslo's urban planning, transportation alternatives, and architectural marvels all reflect the city's commitment to innovation and sustainability. The city's efficient public transportation network, which consists of trams, buses, and ferries, encourages environmentally friendly travel. The Barcode Project, a collection of modern structures, perfectly captures Oslo's innovative spirit and provides the city's skyline a unique appearance.

Locals' Warmth: Oslo's residents, who are famous for their friendliness and knowledge of English, contribute to the city's welcoming atmosphere. Locals are often eager to speak with visitors, share their knowledge, and recommend secret attractions. This social environment fosters a sense of belonging and connection, making visitors feel at home in a foreign nation.

Oslo stands itself as a special tourist destination that wonderfully captures Norway's history, culture, and breathtaking natural surroundings. Its unique blend of historical treasures, contemporary achievements, artistic expressions, and outdoor activities leaves a lasting impact on any visitor who is fortunate enough to see its vibrant streets and serene environs. Oslo ensures that your trip will be a spectacular journey that you will remember long after it is done, whether you want to explore the city's historical sites, savour its mouthwatering food, or enjoy the great outdoors.

Bergen

Bergen is nestled away amid the fjords and mountains on Norway's southwest coast, a wonderful testament to the country's natural beauty and cultural variety. One of the busiest cities in Norway, Bergen, has made a name for itself as a top destination for travellers seeking a seamless mix of history, magnificent beauty, and a vibrant metropolitan culture.

Bergen has a long history that dates back to the eleventh century, and the city's charming wooden houses, meandering streets, and ancient sites give it a timeless feel. The Bryggen Wharf, a UNESCO World Heritage site, is the outstanding example of its old-world beauty.

This colourful row of wooden Hanseatic buildings was built at the height of the Hanseatic League's commercial might. The wharf today offers the perfect combination of traditional and modern with its stores, galleries, and cafés.

For everyone passing through this breathtaking area, Bergen is a must-see location since it serves as the gateway to Norway's well-known fjords. Tourists may easily enjoy fjord cruises and experience the majesty of nature's towering cliffs, gushing waterfalls, and mirror-like waters thanks to the city's near proximity to the well-known Naeroyfjord and Geirangerfjord, both of which are on the UNESCO World Heritage List.

Bergen serves as the focal point of the well-known "Norway in a Nutshell" tour, which also includes a trip on the Flam Railway. An engineering wonder, this railway passes through breathtaking countryside, mountainous slopes, and lush meadows. This journey beautifully captures the variety of Norway's terrain, from snow-capped peaks to serene fjords.

Bergen's vibrant vitality is shown by the plethora of events that fill its cultural calendar. The Bergen International Festival brings together artists from all over the world each year to celebrate music, theatre, dance, and visual arts. The Bergen Food Festival offers visitors the opportunity to indulge in Norway's culinary gems while also tantalising taste buds with a range of regional delicacies.

To view all of Bergen and its breathtaking surroundings, you must take the Floibanen funicular up to Mount Floyen. Wide-ranging views of the city, fjords, and mountains are the reward for ascending the mountain, and they are particularly breathtaking when the midnight sun or Northern Lights are visible.

Bergen has a lot of aquatic adventures to offer since it is a coastline city. While taking a boat tour of the archipelago, tourists may see scenic islands, some of which have modern architecture and others that have traditional wooden houses, and they can also learn about the aquatic life of Norway at the Bergen Aquarium.

The several museums in Bergen serve as a showcase for its rich cultural past. The KODE Art Museums include a sizable collection of art and design from several ages, including works by well-known artists like Edvard Munch. The famed musician Edvard Grieg's life and work are honoured in the Troldhaugen Museum, while Bergen's previous trade is explored at the Hanseatic Museum.

Bergen residents are famous for their gracious hospitality, which contributes to the beauty of the city. By engaging in conversation with folks at the fish market or over a cup of hot coffee, one might learn about their daily life. Be sure to enjoy traditional foods like "klippfisk" (dried and salted fish) and "skillingsboller" (cinnamon buns) for a true taste of Norwegian cuisine.

In conclusion, Bergen is a delightful city that attracts tourists with its historical allure, stunning fjords, vibrant culture, and welcoming residents. Tourists are compelled to immerse themselves in Bergen's timeless beauty and experience everything that Norway has to offer, from the historic Bryggen Wharf to the panoramic vistas of Mount Floyen. Whether you are drawn to Bergen by history, ecology, or culture, it is certainly a top destination that offers lifetime memories and a greater grasp of Norway's attractions.

Tromsø

Tourists seeking both natural beauty and cultural experiences will enjoy visiting Troms, which is situated within the Arctic Circle. Due to its magnificent beauty, vibrant displays of the northern lights, rich indigenous heritage, and modern urban comforts, Troms is without a doubt one of Norway's top tourist attractions. Every traveller will find this Arctic gem to be rich in attractions, from its breath-taking natural wonders to its enjoyable urban activities.

Troms's natural beauty is really breathtaking. The city is surrounded by magnificent fjords, snow-capped mountains, and beautiful canals, which provide an amazing setting for amazing activities. Hikers may go along paths like the well-known Fjellheisen cable car, which offers panoramic views of the city and its stunning surroundings. While taking in the snowy wonderland, visitors may engage in exhilarating winter activities like dog sledding, snowmobiling, and cross-country skiing.

The Aurora Borealis, often known as the northern lights, are frequently hailed as one of the finest sights to view, and Troms is no exception. Tourists go to this Arctic region in the winter to see the vibrant green, pink, and purple hues blazing across the night sky. The Northern Lights Observatory offers the opportunity to learn more about the phenomenon and the physics that underlie it, adding a more educational component to the beautiful experience.

The Sami people have lived in the Arctic for many centuries, and Troms gives visitors a chance to engage with their rich cultural heritage. The Sami Cultural Center exhibits traditions, artwork, and handicrafts to visitors. Traditional Sami cuisine and reindeer sledding add to the authenticity of the cultural interaction and provide tourists a unique glimpse into the way of life there.

Despite its seclusion, Troms has a vibrant city feel. The city's lively markets, modern comforts, and crowded cafés give it a cosmopolitan vibe that elegantly contrasts with the surrounding natural nature. The Arctic Cathedral, a stunning building that resembles an ice sculpture, is a unique landmark that adds to Troms' urban attraction. Visitors may learn about the habitats, creatures, and environmental problems affecting the Arctic at the Polaria Arctic Experience Center by combining education and fun.

The city of Troms has a bustling artistic and cultural scene all year round. The city hosts several theatre performances, music festivals, and exhibitions to showcase local talent as well as those from across the globe. The Troms International Film Festival increases the city's cultural offerings by attracting cinema fans from all over the world.

In addition to its own charms, Troms serves as a launching place for further Arctic adventures. Travellers may go on expeditions to Svalbard to witness polar bears in their natural habitat or take icebreaker excursions into the Arctic tundra. Due to its favourable location, Troms is a fantastic place to start for anyone searching for more difficult sports.

The city of Troms, which sits in the heart of Norway's Arctic region, draws tourists with its stunning landscape, captivating displays of the northern lights, rich indigenous heritage, urban charm, and vibrant arts scene. This well-liked tourist destination provides a once-in-a-lifetime experience that expertly combines the wonders of nature with cultural immersion, leaving a lasting effect on everyone who visits this Arctic jewel. No matter whether you're a nature lover, a cultural traveller, or an adventure seeker, Troms is a must-see destination that ensures a fascinating journey into the heart of the Arctic environment.

Trondheim

Along the stunning Trondheimsfjord coastline sits Trondheim, a timeless city with a vibrant cultural scene, a deep history, and stunning surroundings. Due to its mediaeval magnificence, modern comforts, and seamless blending of the old and new, Trondheim emerges as a favourite destination for tourists heading into the heart of Norway.

There are many historical relics in Trondheim, which was founded in 997 AD by the Viking King Olav Tryggvason. The Nidaros Cathedral, one of the most well-known specimens of Gothic architecture, serves as a powerful illustration of the city's spiritual significance. The intricate carvings and stunning structures have drawn pilgrims here since the dawn of time, and they continue to inspire adoration in them.

Beautiful landscapes: Trondheim's natural beauty enchants visitors all year long. It is surrounded by rolling hills, thick woodlands, and peaceful canals. The Nidelva River is beautifully seen from the charming Gamle Bybro (Old Town Bridge), and the Bymarka woods offer opportunities for trekking and skiing. The stunning Trondheimsfjord offers sailing, kayaking, and fishing adventures.

Trondheim vibrant arts scene serves as evidence of its cultural vibrancy. The city's many museums and galleries showcase mediaeval antiquities, contemporary artwork, and Viking artefacts to study its past. The Rockheim museum honours Norway's musical heritage by tracing its evolution from traditional folk music to modern pop.

Education Center: The renowned Norwegian University of Science and Technology (NTNU), located in Trondheim, draws academics and students from all over the globe. The city is revitalised and encouraged to be creative by the influx of young minds, and the university campus itself is a hive of innovative concepts and cutting-edge design.

Streets in the city are lined with colourful wooden houses that exude a distinct Nordic charm. The charming Bakklandet and Ila neighbourhoods of Trondheim, which contain small cafés, boutiques, and antique stores, provide an insight into local life.

culinary Delights: The gourmet scene in Trondheim is worth exploring. The city is well known for emphasising the use of locally sourced ingredients, which results in delectable dishes that respect Norwegian culture. Visitors may experience the regional specialties at a variety of restaurants, including fresh seafood and reindeer meat.

Festivals and Events: Trondheim is vibrant all year long thanks to a wide range of vibrant festivals and events. With performances, processions, and cultural events, the St. Olav Festival celebrates the city's patron saint. Film lovers are drawn to the city by both the Christmas market and the Trondheim International Film Festival (Kosmorama).

Accessibility: Thanks to an efficient public transportation system, travellers can easily reach Trondheim. Travellers from all over the world are welcomed at the Trondheim Airport Vaernes, which also links the city to significant international hubs. Exploring the city and its surroundings is also made simple by the efficient public transit system.

Due to its intriguing fusion of history, nature, culture, and modernity, Trondheim will appeal to those looking for a true Norwegian experience. The Nidaros Cathedral's soaring spires and the tranquillity of the Trondheimsfjord are just two of the many features of this city that call for exploration and discovery. Whether you're a fan of history, nature, or culture, Trondheim gives a remarkable glimpse into the heart of Norway's richness.

Chapter 4. Exploring Nature

Fjords and Waterfalls

Norway's pristine landscapes and amazing natural attractions have traditionally made it a haven for travellers seeking to get in touch with nature. Among its many attractions, fjords and waterfalls stand out as some of the most magnificent and beautiful places. With its unique blend of untamed beauty, calm tranquillity, and exciting adventure, this Scandinavian gem draws nature enthusiasts from all over the world.

The largest works of art created by nature are commonly referred to as fjords, which are geological formations that have been carved by glaciers over millions of years. The stunning landscape and towering cliffs that surround these narrow, deep water inlets captivate tourists to no end. A handful of Norway's well-known fjords include the famed Geirangerfjord, Naeroyfjord, and Sognefjord, all of which have been designated UNESCO World Heritage Sites.

The Geirangerfjord in western Norway is said to be Norway's best fjord. Its emerald-green waters are surrounded by towering cliffs that seem to approach the heavens. Two waterfalls that cascade down the slopes of the fjord are The Seven Sisters and The Suitor, adding to the ethereal magnificence of the area. A trip to Geirangerfjord offers a close experience with nature and the chance to see the beauty of its well sculpted landscape.

A smaller, to the side branch of the Sognefjord called Naeroyfjord offers a more private fjord experience. A pleasant and serene atmosphere is created by its stunning scenery, which includes steep mountain sides covered with thick vegetation. The fjord winds through the countryside, passing through quaint settlements that give visitors a glimpse of Norway's traditional way of life.

Sognefjord, sometimes referred to as the King of Fjords, is the longest and deepest fjord in Norway. The beauty of its surroundings is the only thing that comes close to matching its awe-inspiring magnitude. The fjord's shores are dotted with tumbling waterfalls, lush valleys, and charming settlements, offering a wide range of leisure and exploring opportunities. The Flm Railway, one of the world's most scenic rail journeys, provides an unrivalled vantage point to take in the splendour of the fjord.

The fjords of Norway include some of the most stunning waterfalls on earth. These untamed wonders, whose powers vary from tranquil streams of water to violent waterfalls, add to the splendour of the surroundings. The 600-foot-tall Voringsfossen waterfall, which flows down a vertical cliff, is a breathtaking sight to see. The deafening boom and misty spray of the cascade leave visitors in awe at nature's might.

The Hardangervidda plateau's centre is home to a group of beautiful waterfalls known as the

Tyssestrengene waterfalls, which flow over rocky terrain. The unpolluted landscapes and clean waters provide a tranquil setting for reflection and relaxation. Adventure-seeking travellers will love hikes that lead to undiscovered gems like the Langfossen waterfall, where flowing water gracefully cascades over the incline.

Exploring Norway's fjords and waterfalls involves more than simply admiring the scenery. The country offers a broad variety of outdoor activities that enable tourists to fully appreciate the wonders of nature. While kayaking among the spectacular cliffs and serene coves of the fjords, adventurers may experience these sights. From leisurely strolls to difficult adventures, hiking paths wind through breathtaking landscapes and provide breathtaking views at every turn.

For the traveller looking for adventure, there are several opportunities for heart-pounding thrill. Cliff diving into the clear fjord waters, paragliding over the fjord valleys, or even ice climbing in the winter are all intriguing ways to take in the region. Because of the contrast between beautiful beauty and exhilarating activities, Norway is a refuge for adventurers.

When visiting Norway's fjords and waterfalls, one may marvel at the beauty of nature and discover peace and quiet away from the hustle and bustle of the city. Because of their astounding beauty and serenity, these natural wonders will leave a lasting imprint on your soul, whether you're standing on a cliff, gazing at a majestic waterfall, or sailing over calm waters. In Norway, fjords and waterfalls serve as more than just tourist attractions; they open doors to a deeper understanding of the grandeur and majesty of nature.

National Parks

Norway's National Parks are a testament to the country's commitment to safeguarding its unique ecosystems and providing tourists with an unrivalled opportunity to see nature in its most untainted condition. They are hidden away among unspoiled beauty and a wealth of natural wonders. With their diverse landscapes, stunning fjords, towering mountains, and an abundance of species, Norway's National Parks provide a haven for travellers, hikers, wildlife enthusiasts, and anybody seeking a closer connection to nature.

1. National Parks in Norway: A Gem of Scandinavian Nature

With a broad network of national parks, Norway is home to a wide range of environments, from the high Arctic to the coast. The Norwegian government established more than 40 national parks, covering more than 15,000 square kilometres, to protect the country's natural heritage. Each park offers a different perspective on Norway's unparalleled ecosystems and landscapes.

2. Examining the Spectacular Fjords and Coastlines

Fjords are among the most identifiable natural features in Norway, and several national parks provide excellent vantage points for viewing these magnificent geological formations. Parks like Jotunheimen, located in the centre of Norway, provide tourists access to stunning fjords like Sognefjord and Geirangerfjord, where they may hike, sail, or just admire the wonders of nature.

3. The Call of the Mountains

The harsh terrain of Norway is dominated by magnificent mountains, and various national parks are havens for climbers, hikers, and mountaineers. Parks like Rondane and Hardangervidda are widely recognized for their peaks and broad plateaus and provide trails for hikers of all ability levels. From these heights, one may enjoy spectacular views of the countryside that go all the way to the horizon.

4. The Arctic Wonders

As they go farther north, they could reach the Arctic, where national parks like Svalbard provide a rare opportunity to experience the arid conditions of the north. Svalbard's beautiful landscapes are home to arctic foxes, reindeer, and polar bears. Visitors may participate in organised excursions or guided tours to see a location where the sun never sets throughout the summer.

5. Sightings of Wildlife

In addition to stunning landscapes, Norwegian National Parks are home to a diversity of unusual animals. National parks like Dovrefjell-Sunndalsfjella are where you can observe the unusual musk oxen, while other parks are where you can see rare bird species and marine life. Photographers and wildlife enthusiasts can get transfixed by these unusual creatures' immobility.

6. Adapting the Norwegian idea of "Allemannsrett"

The concept of "allemannsrett," or "everyman's right," plays a crucial role in how Norwegians perceive their national parks. Due to this unique legal privilege, everyone enjoys access to practically all of Norway's rural areas, including national parks. Travellers are allowed to camp, walk, and enjoy the outdoors in a responsible manner while removing all signs of their stay and contributing to the preservation of these stunning surroundings.

7. Ecotourism and environmental preservation

As the need for sustainable travel becomes more widely recognized, Norway's National Parks have taken steps to ensure that tourism doesn't degrade the same environment it wants to promote. There are regulations in place to reduce traffic, maintain cleanliness, and safeguard the parks' delicate ecosystems.

8. Selecting a National Park in Norway for Your Adventure

Whether you're a seasoned traveller or a novice, seeing Norway's National Parks requires careful planning. Do your research on any parks that catch your attention, dress appropriately for unpredictable weather, and abide by any guidelines that the park management may have imposed. Consider hiring expert local guides if you want to travel securely and discover new things.

9. The National Parks of Norway and Their Everlasting Allure

In a world of constantly changing landscapes, Norway's National Parks stand as timeless havens where nature keeps its prominent position. Their allure comes not only from the beautiful views they provide, but also from the opportunity to get away from the hustle and bustle of everyday life and reconnect with the wonders of the world. Visitors seeking a close touch with nature are invited to visit Norway's National Parks.

10. Exploration All Year Round: Seasons of Wonder

Norway's National Parks provide year-round access to their wonder, which is not confined to any one season. The summertime brings vibrant flora, flowing waterfalls, and busy wildlife to the parks, bringing them to life. As autumn paints the landscapes in warm hues, hikers are greeted to a symphony of colours that is nothing short of breathtaking. In the winter, the parks are transformed into a snow-covered wonderland, ideal for cross-country skiing, snowshoeing, and in certain parks farther north, even getting a glimpse of the spectacular Northern Lights.

11. Stunning Cultural Heritage

Norway's national parks are not only stunning in the natural world, but they also have a lot of cultural significance. Several parks have historical sites that tell stories about the people who formerly called these remote areas home. Traditional Sami culture is included into the parks in the northern regions, providing tourists with the chance to learn about the indigenous people who have coexisted peacefully and sustainably with nature for millennia.

12. The Gateway to Exploration

The National Parks of Norway provide a wide range of thrilling activities for the adventurous traveller. For those seeking heart-pounding thrills, the parks provide a playground with pursuits like ice climbing frozen waterfalls in Romsdalen and kayaking in the fjords of Jotunheimen. These activities provide a unique perspective on Norway's landscapes that observation alone cannot.

13. All Accessible

Even though some of Norway's National Parks are remote and difficult to enter, many of them are open to visitors of all ages and fitness levels. Thanks to well-marked paths and accommodation choices that range from modest hotels to comfortable cottages, everybody can take in the beauty and tranquillity of these natural treasures.

14. A distinctive practice is nature therapy.

Being in nature has several documented health advantages, making Norway's National Parks the perfect setting for a rejuvenating vacation. Whether you're looking for solitude, want to unplug, or simply need a break from the busy pace of life, the parks provide a setting that fosters relaxation, awareness, and a deep sense of connection to the Earth.

15. Promotion of Environmental awareness.

Norway encourages environmental protection by allowing tourists to visit its national parks. After seeing the beauty and fragility of these habitats firsthand, visitors are often inspired to become fervent advocates of environmental conservation both at home and abroad.

16. A Way of Self-Realisation

A journey of self-discovery is as much a part of visiting Norway's National Parks as it is a physical one. Whether you're negotiating treacherous terrain, taking in breath-blowing beauty, or coming across strange species, these experiences have a powerful way of altering attitudes and instilling a sense of humility and surprise.

17. Leaving a Legacy

Even when tourists leave Norway's National Parks and return to their daily lives, their influence endures. Their memories of peaceful strolls through ancient woodlands, the rush of fresh mountain air, and the beauty of unspoilt panoramas will serve as a constant reminder of the need of conserving our natural environment for future generations.

18. Stories Unwritten

No matter how much is said and written about Norway's National Parks, there will always be untold stories waiting to be found by those who go into their depths. The rustle of animals in the underbrush, the whisper of the wind through the trees, and the dance of sunlight on still lakes are among the symphony of feelings that can only be completely understood by those who go off the beaten path and immerse themselves in nature.

In conclusion, Norway's National Parks are more than simply tourist attractions; they are gateways to a world of natural splendour, diverse cultures, and personal growth. From the arid highlands to the icy Arctic wastes, each park depicts a unique feature of Norway's various environments. Visitors seeking a genuine and deep connection with nature are invited to go on an extraordinary journey of exploration and self-discovery in these parks.

Northern Lights Viewing

Natural wonders like the Aurora Borealis, sometimes known as the Northern Lights, have long captivated travellers and explorers. Due to Norway's clever positioning within the Arctic Circle, tourists have a rare opportunity to see this magnificent phenomena. People from all over the globe come to this Scandinavian gem to see the once-in-a-lifetime spectacle of dazzling colours dancing across the night sky.

For those seeking to really experience the beauty of nature, Norway's Northern Lights viewing is unparalleled. The untouched and remote landscapes, which provide an ethereal aura that is both modest and inspiring, serve as a good framing for this heavenly sight.

The best time to observe the Northern Lights in Norway is during the winter, which lasts from September to March. It is simple to observe the ethereal lights at this time due to the darkness and clear sky. One of the most popular places to see the Northern Lights is Troms, also referred to as the "Gateway to the Arctic." The many events and hotel choices in this bustling city are aimed towards Northern Lights enthusiasts.

Tourists may select from a number of activities to make the most of their trip to see the Northern Lights. There is something for everyone, from guided tours that take you to fantastic observation locations to exciting dog sledding or snowmobile experiences. Consider travelling on a dog sled over a tundra blanketed in snow while the Northern Lights display dazzling hues of green, pink, and purple in the sky. The only noises are the soft footsteps of people and an occasional wind whisper.

If you want to see the Northern Lights in peace, a wilderness resort in a remote location could be your best bet. Since they are situated outside of the busy metropolis, these cabins provide a sense of solitude and serenity that is becoming harder and harder to obtain in today's world. Imagine yourself lounging by a cosy fireplace, wrapped in a plush blanket, and enjoying the stars dancing for you outside the window.

Photographers will also feel at ease while capturing the Northern Lights in Norway. It is possible to capture spectacular and unique images due to the sheer intensity and diversity of colours. Whether you're a beginner using a smartphone or a professional utilising top-notch equipment, the Northern Lights will undoubtedly be the focus of your portfolio.

Although Norway's natural beauty extends beyond the night sky, the Northern Lights continue to be its biggest attraction. Throughout the day, tourists may come across breathtaking fjords, snow-capped mountains, and attractive coastal towns. Skiing, fjord cruises, and Sami cultural tours all contribute to a well-rounded experience that highlights the diversity of this Nordic nation.

In conclusion, Norway is a great destination for those seeking a particularly special experience to see the Northern Lights. Due to its location, gorgeous scenery, and variety of activities, it is a popular choice for both nature enthusiasts and adventurers. The Northern Lights' mysterious and mesmerising dance creates a connection between Earth and sky that is an authentic witness to the wonders of the natural world. Everyone who travels to Norway to see this wonderful beauty will keep it in their hearts and minds for the rest of their lives.

Chapter 5. Cultural Experiences

Norwegian Cuisine

Visitors may enjoy a unique culinary experience in Norway that reflects the country's history, geography, and traditions. Beautiful fjords, bustling cities, and a strong cultural heritage may all be found throughout the nation. Fresh and locally produced ingredients are heavily emphasised in Norwegian cuisine. Learning about Norwegian food allows visitors to participate in the traditions and flavours of this Nordic nation in addition to being a gourmet experience.

Norwegian food: A Taste of Tradition and Nature Introduction

Old traditions and modern ideas come together in the delectable variety of Norwegian cuisine, which is delicately entwined with the wealth of

Norway's wild landscapes. The gastronomic character of Norway is greatly influenced by its distinctive environment, which spans from coastal fishing villages to lush inland areas. As they embark on their journey through this wonderful continent, visitors are greeted with a variety of flavours, each of which narrates a narrative of tenacity, innovation, and tradition.

A Love Affair with the Ocean: Seafood's Vitality

For millennia, the coastal residents of Norway have depended on the sea for subsistence. Seafood is a mainstay of Norwegian cuisine, particularly fish like haddock, cod, and salmon. Visitors may enjoy the best seafood cuisine, which ranges from simple smoked salmon on open-faced sandwiches to the renowned lutefisk, which is made of dried and rehydrated fish treated with lye. Unconventional eaters may also appreciate rakfisk, a dish of fermented fish with cultural significance that is often offered during celebrations.

Preservation Techniques: A Nod to Custom and Need

Because of the harsh winters in Norway and the need to preserve food for a long time, the employment of preservation methods including drying, salting, and fermenting has long been a mainstay of Norwegian cuisine. Tourists have the opportunity to learn more about these cultural practices via dishes like klippfisk (dried and salted fish) and surströmming (fermented herring). These age-old techniques show how skillfully Norwegians can use the natural world's resources to sustain themselves all year long.

Celebrating Ingredients: From Farm to Table

Visitors may enjoy the flavours of Norway's beautiful valleys and rolling hills by sourcing nearby inland. Local elements including potatoes, root vegetables, and berries take prominent roles in dishes like raspeballer (potato dumplings) and multekrem (cloudberry cream). The fact that so many restaurants and cafés in Norway proudly get their ingredients from local farmers and producers shows how well-established the farm-to-table concept is in Norwegian culture.

Foraging: The Wild Harvest on Your Plate

Foraging, a cherished Norwegian tradition, enables guests to come closer to nature's wealth. The meals are made richer and with a sense of the wild thanks to the diversity of wild mushrooms, berries, and herbs that are provided by the forests. Norwegian dishes include forest flavours like chanterelles and cloudberries.

A Look Into Tradition: Examining Food Festivals

Travellers might time their vacation to coincide with one of the many culinary festivals held there in order to learn more about Norwegian culture and cuisine. The Bergen Fish Market Festival celebrates Norway's maritime heritage while showcasing fish and local cuisine. Fans of the tasty fermented fish dish gather in Trondheim for the annual RakfiskFestival for a memorable meal. These occasions provide the opportunity to socialise, learn about traditional cooking methods, and celebrate the essence of Norwegian culture in addition to eating delicious food.

Innovation and Fusion: Contemporary Approaches to Tradition

Norwegian cuisine respects its cultural heritage while embracing contemporary culinary trends and foreign influences. In cosmopolitan cities like Oslo, tourists may find a diverse dining scene that includes everything from traditional Norwegian food to global fusion. A culinary landscape that celebrates the past while embracing the present has resulted from renowned chefs reworking traditional dishes with cutting-edge preparation techniques and displays.

A Culinary Expedition Through Norway's Heart and Soul

The cuisine of Norway, which blends aspects of tradition, geography, and history, may provide tourists with a comprehensive cultural experience. Every meal is an opportunity to experience the spirit of the nation, whether it originates in the lush valleys or the beach towns. Through seafood-rich feasts, preservation techniques, locally produced delicacies, foraging excursions, and culinary festivals, tourists may go on a sensory journey that not only fills the palate but also provides a look into the spirit of Norway's people and surroundings. Learning about Norwegian cuisine is a cultural experience that nourishes the mind, body, and spirit, whether you like cutting-edge innovations or centuries-old traditions.

Traditional Festivals

Attending one of Norway's traditional festivals provides visitors with a unique opportunity to thoroughly appreciate the country's rich cultural past. Instead of just being events, these festivities provide glimpses into the profoundly rooted customs, beliefs, and aspirations that characterised the Norwegian way of life. Travellers may participate in the vibrant festivals that showcase the soul and spirit of Norway's cultural tapestry as they pass through the breathtaking fjords, mountains, and quaint towns that make up the country's scenery.

One of Norway's most well-known and much anticipated holidays is Syttende Mai, or National Day, which is observed on May 17th each year. This day marks the adoption of the Norwegian Constitution in 1814 as a symbol of the nation's independence and unity. Streets are lined with flags, and locals dress in "bunads," or traditional garb. Visitors are often encouraged to take part in the celebratory parades, waving Norwegian flags and soaking in the tremendous sense of patriotism in the air. With children's processions and plays, the day comes to a close with a spirit of kindness that personifies Norway.

Visitors visiting Norway have the chance to enjoy the beauty of enduring Yuletide rituals throughout the Christmas season. The "Jul" celebrations are heavily rooted in Norse mythology and paganism. Tourists may visit locations like Oslo and Bergen to see the amazing Christmas markets, which offer traditional crafts, local delicacies, and the cosy glow of holiday lights. Two of the most cherished traditions include lighting Advent candles and exhibiting lovely wooden "nisser," mythical creatures said to guard houses. Additionally, because cross-country skiing and the Norwegian love of skiing go hand in hand, tournaments are often organised throughout this season.

Another occasion that draws travellers seeking authentic cultural encounters is the St. Olav's Festival, which celebrates Olav II, the patron saint of Norway. This event successfully combines music with art, faith with history. Visitors and pilgrims alike are welcome to attend religious services, plays, talks, and guided tours. The celebration honours both the country's historical ties to the Viking age and its Christian history, providing a thorough experience that caters to a wide range of interests.

Entering the realm of myth and magic, the Midsummer's Eve or "Sankthansaften" event honours the enigmatic allure of the midnight sun. This festival, which is held on June 23, is well-known for its many bonfires beside the water. In order to ward off evil spirits and provide good luck, visitors are allowed to take part in traditional ceremonies that involve dancing, singing, and leaping over flames. When the sun briefly dips below the horizon, the ethereal light produces an atmosphere that is highly captivating.

The Norsk RakfiskFestival is a culinary delight that displays Norway's relationship to its aquatic environment. Rakfisk, or fermented fish, has been a mainstay of Norwegian cuisine for ages. During this occasion, visitors may sample a variety of this regional food, discover how it is made, and speak with local fishermen in the town of Fagernes. Tradition and modernity, as well as the past and present, are brought together via a sensory experience.

Finally, unlike ordinary tourist destinations, Norway's traditional festivals provide access to cultural contacts that enrich travel experiences. These events are actualized representations of Norway's history, values, and traditions and provide visitors an opportunity to interact more thoroughly with locals. Every celebration, from the joyous parades of Syttende Mai to the ethereal allure of Midsummer's Eve, adds another piece to the mosaic of Norwegian identity. In addition to creating cherished memories, tourists who take part in these celebrations contribute to preserving Norway's rich cultural heritage for future generations.

Viking History

Walking across Norway's breathtaking landscapes instantly takes tourists to the Viking Age, a time of bold sailor and intrepid explorers. The rich history of the Vikings is entrenched in the very fabric of the nation and provides an unrivalled cultural experience for those who are interested in diving into the intriguing world of raiding, trading, and exploration. Norway provides a unique opportunity to fully immerse oneself in the Norse legacy that changed the course of European history, from the energetic city of Oslo to the serene fjords and historic sites dotting the countryside. This page gives you a tour of Viking history by combining the accounts of their artistic achievements, maritime prowess, and ongoing influence on modern Norway.

1. The Viking Age: Evolution and Propagation
The Viking Age, roughly from the late eighth to the early eleventh century, was a period of significant upheaval in Scandinavian history. A multitude of factors, including population growth, improvements in shipbuilding

technology, and a thirst for adventure, led to the legendary Viking voyages. They originated in the modern nations of Denmark, Norway, and Sweden, and ultimately spread their influence to far-off locales like Iceland, Greenland, the British Isles, and even North America.

2. Seafaring prowess and the legacy of longships

The foundation of the Vikings' experience was their mastery in shipbuilding. The Norsemen were able to navigate crowded rivers and wide oceans with astonishing ease because of the famed longships' shallow drafts and streamlined design. Along with assisting their raids and conquests, this nautical technology opened the way for lucrative trade routes, connecting distant regions and fostering cultural exchanges. Visitors may learn about the technological marvels that allowed the Vikings to explore new seas while marvelling at the beautifully rebuilt longships at historical sites and museums all around Norway.

3. Viking culture and society

The Vikings were renowned for their skill at sea, as well as their stunning artwork, extensive oral traditions, and unique social systems. Visitors visiting Norway may completely immerse themselves in Viking culture with interactive museums that include everything from mediaeval clothing and weaponry to runic inscriptions and religious relics. The concept of a "Thing" provides a window into their system of administration, which puts a significant emphasis on the participation of free men in social matters. A "Thing" was a democratic assembly where decisions were made collectively.

4. The Influence of Norse Mythology

Viking culture was based on the Norse pantheon of gods, which included Odin, Thor, and Freyja. In addition to being deities to be revered, these gods provided inspiration for literature, art, and stories. Visitors may engage with this enchanted aspect of Viking history by learning about ancient tales and sagas that continue to influence modern literature and entertainment. Further evidence of Norse mythology's ongoing spiritual importance may be seen in Norway's stunning stave churches. These structures are ornamented with intricate sculptures of mythological themes.

5. Monuments and archaeological wonders

Travellers may discover a plethora of archaeological sites all around Norway that provide intriguing insights into Viking civilization. The exquisitely preserved burial vessel known as the Oseberg Ship, which was discovered in a mound not far from Oslo, is an example of the riches and talent of the Viking royalty. In addition to interactive exhibits, authentic attire, and hands-on activities, the Lofotr Viking Museum in the Lofoten Islands allows visitors to explore a replica of a Viking chieftain's longhouse. These websites provide users the ability to experience Viking life and trace their movements.

6. Cultural resonance and modernization

The Vikings' enduring impact may still be felt today, as seen by the language, culture, and way of life in modern Norway. This linguistic heritage is commonly mentioned in regional dialects. The Norwegian language itself has remnants of Old Norse, the language of the Vikings. To honour the craftsmanship of the Viking age, modern artisans produce wonderful jewellery, textiles, and woodwork. Through festivals, reenactments, and historical recreations, visitors may further immerse themselves in the vibrant Viking cultural echoes that continue to shape Norway's character.

The opportunity to engage with a living heritage that has significantly shaped Norway's culture and customs is provided through a journey through its Viking history. From the rocky Norwegian coast to the stunning fjords and well run museums, every region of the country offers a unique window into the fascinating world of the Norsemen. Whether visitors choose to learn about the intricate designs of longships or delve into the sagas of mighty warriors, they will undoubtedly be enthralled by the captivating saga of the Vikings, a cultural experience that transcends time and leaves an enduring imprint on their understanding of this remarkable period in history.

Chapter 6. Outdoor Activities

Hiking and Trekking

Trekking and hiking provide unequalled opportunities to enjoy nature's raw magnificence in this Nordic wonderland. Due to the diversity of its environment, which includes fjords, mountains, forests, and glaciers, Norway offers a wide choice of hiking and trekking experiences that are suited for tourists of all skill levels. Whether you're a seasoned climber or a novice nature lover, Norway's trails are simply waiting to be explored.

Norway's Magnificent Terrain :
Norway's diverse environment provides an endless variety of hiking and trekking options. Its most recognized feature is without a doubt its fjords, vast inlets with sheer walls formed by glaciers over millions of years. The fjords provide a unique landscape for hiking trails with

breathtaking views. On hikes like the Trolltunga and Preikestolen, which lead to breath-taking vistas that overlook these geological treasures, hikers may feel awe and accomplishment.

Adventure Hiking for All Levels of Experience : For beginners, Norway provides a selection of easy pathways that meander through lovely woodlands and serene meadows. Visitors may enjoy a leisurely hike that allows them to take in the scenery at a leisurely pace on trails like the Rallarvegen. Your stamina will be put to the test on trails like Besseggen, which become harder as you ascend and reward you with panoramic vistas of the glacier-carved valleys and beautiful lakes of Jotunheimen National Park.

Experienced hikers will relish the opportunity to attempt more difficult trails like the Arctic Circle Trail. On this trek into the untamed nature of Northern Norway, trekkers may see the ethereal Northern Lights throughout the whole winter. The Hardangervidda Plateau, the highest mountain plateau in Europe, offers another intriguing challenge with its pathways that cross extensive moorlands and exhibit the wild beauty of Norwegian nature.

What Hiking Can Give You in Norway :
In Norway, hiking is more than just finishing a route; it's also about taking in the scenery and appreciating the trip. The country is committed to preserving its natural beauty, thus hiking trails are maintained in high shape and provide a spotless experience. Due to the "Allemannsrett," or "everyman's right," which permits camping and exploration in most uninhabited areas, hikers may really connect with their surroundings and enjoy a sense of calm that is rare to find elsewhere.

How to Get Ready :
When preparing for a hiking or trekking adventure in Norway, the right gear must be packed. A reliable backpack, reliable hiking boots, adequate clothing for the weather, and other safety equipment are requirements. It is suggested to layer your clothing since Norway's

weather might be unpredictable in order to be comfortable while visiting. When travelling to far-off places, it's also essential to carry equipment like a map, compass, first aid kit, extra food, and water.

Respecting the environment and local culture :
While exploring Norway's trails, it is crucial to act responsibly as a visitor. Respecting the environment and local culture is essential. Stick to known channels to minimise ecological impact and avoid disturbing animals. Follow the "Leave No Trace" principles as a visitor in this pristine area to ensure that future generations may take delight in the same unspoilt beauty.

Organising Your Adventure :
Before beginning a hiking or trekking expedition in Norway, preparation is essential. Before you travel, learn more about the trail's difficulty rating, the predicted weather, and other important details. Consider the season as well; although summer offers longer daylight hours, winter provides the opportunity to see the

splendour of the Northern Lights. Additionally, if you want to embark on multi-day treks, it is highly encouraged to book arrangements for accomodation in advance.

In Norway, going on a hike or a journey allows you to connect closely with nature while exploring new places. With its magnificent landscape, interesting excursions, and commitment to maintaining its natural beauty, Norway entices tourists to experience its wild environment. Norway's outdoor activities provide a remarkable experience, whether you're a novice hiker searching for leisurely strolls or an expert trekker keen to take on challenging terrains. Put your hiking boots on, gather your supplies, and go off to see the intriguing world of Norwegian hiking and trekking.

Skiing and Winter Sports

In the middle of Scandinavia, Norway is a winter paradise for travellers and nature enthusiasts seeking exhilarating pursuits in the snow-covered landscapes. Norway offers an attractive backdrop for a broad range of winter sports and activities that are appropriate for individuals of all skill and experience levels thanks to its stunning fjords, unspoilt woodlands, and towering mountains. From the thrill of downhill skiing to the tranquillity of cross-country paths, Norway encourages tourists to enjoy the beauty of its winter paradise.

Skiing Downhill in Norway and Defying Gravity :

For both seasoned skiers and adrenaline junkies, Norway's alpine ski resorts are a skier's heaven. In locations like Hemsedal, Trysil, and Geilo, there are several well-groomed slopes, challenging runs, and modern services. One of the largest ski resorts in the country is Trysil, and Hemsedal's wide terrain is recognized for its variety. Geilo offers a unique mix of slopes that are appropriate for beginners and difficult terrain thanks to its attractive village backdrop. These resorts not only provide fantastic skiing opportunities, but also breathtaking vistas of snow-covered valleys and sparkling ice lakes.

Cross-country skiing: Finding Peace in the Norwegian Wilderness

For those seeking a more peaceful connection with nature, cross-country skiing provides a close engagement with Norway's winter landscape. Skiers may go on the sophisticated network of groomed trails, or "loipes," deep into Norway's magnificent landscapes, across frozen lakes, and through snow-covered woodlands. The Birkebeinerrennet, a 54-kilometre cross-country ski marathon that draws participants from all over the globe, is a prime example of the attraction of this age-old winter sport.

Snowshoeing and Winter Hiking in Norway: A Quiet Beauty

Snowshoeing and winter trekking open up a world of options for those who seek to fully immerse themselves in Norway's stunning snowscapes without the need for specialised equipment or significant expertise. The spectacular landscapes of Jotunheimen National Park and the ethereal ambiance of the Arctic tundra may all be seen up close when participating in these activities, which provide a glimpse into Norway's winter paradise.

Dog Sledding: A Time Travel Adventure

Dog sledding, a practice deeply established in Norwegian culture, is available to tourists who want to experience an authentic Arctic journey. Participants go over snow-covered trails being escorted by a team of huskies, taking in the breathtaking majesty of Norway's northern regions. The gentle jingle of harnesses and the rhythmic sound of paws on snow as you cross ice meadows create a magical atmosphere.

Getting into the Frozen Waters of Norway to Go Ice Fishing :

Ice fishing is a unique way to experience Norway's winter splendour. When the lakes freeze over, anglers may drill holes in the ice to fish for trout, char, and other natural species. The calm surroundings and the thrill of the catch make for a really unique outdoor experience.

Following the northern lights: the celestial winter show

Even though it's not a sport, seeing the Northern Lights adds a distinctive touch to every winter journey to Norway. The finest locations to see this fascinating phenomenon are in the Arctic regions, including Troms, Kirkenes, and Alta. The breathtaking and otherworldly experience of pursuing the illusive dance of colours across the night sky will stay with travellers forever.

Taking to the skies to see Norway's beauty throughout the winter :

For those who are very courageous, winter paragliding gives a unique perspective of Norway's snow-covered landscapes. When paragliders take off from snow-covered slopes and fly over picturesque valleys, they experience a combination of excitement and awe.

In conclusion, Norway offers a broad range of experiences that satisfy every traveller's need for adventure and a feeling of connection with nature via its winter sports and outdoor activities. When you're ready to succumb to its allure, Norway's snow-covered heaven awaits, providing everything from the exciting rush of downhill skiing to the tranquil calm of cross-country trails. Whether you're a seasoned tourist or athlete, a trip through Norway's winter wonderland will take you into its breathtaking natural beauty.

Coastal Cruises

Among the outdoor activities offered to visitors in Norway, coastal cruises stand out since they provide a unique experience. Adventurers and nature lovers are welcome to go on thrilling adventures along Norway's beaches, which are dotted with fjords, islands, and stunning landscapes. In addition to the opportunity to see the breathtaking scenery of the nation, coastal excursions provide a unique viewpoint on the nation's rich maritime history and culture.

Examining the Fjords:
Fjords are inland inlets that are deep and narrow that were carved out by glaciers. Norway is widely recognized for its fjords. A coastline cruise is a wonderful way to get a close-up look at these natural wonders. One of the most well-known fjords is the Geirangerfjord, a UNESCO World Heritage site noted for its soaring cliffs, cascading waterfalls, and serene blue waters. Passengers on cruise ships may see the magnificence of these fjords from a vantage point that is unequalled by exploration on land.

trips to other islands:

With more than 50,000 islands along its coast, Norway provides an island-hopping paradise for anybody looking for outdoor pleasures. Tourists may uncover unknown gems, remote fishing villages, and tranquil coves in these scattered isles, which are sailed by coastal boats. The stunning peaks and vibrant fishing communities of the Lofoten Islands make them a must-visit destination for anybody on a coastal cruise. To understand more about Norway's marine heritage and symbiotic relationship with the sea, these islands may be visited.

interactions with animals:

Norway's coastal waters are teeming with a variety of marine life, making the country's coastal excursions a haven for nature lovers. From the comfort of a cruise ship, tourists may see whales, dolphins, seals, and a variety of birdlife. The chance to see these creatures in their natural habitat is breathtaking and leaves a lasting impact.

immersion in cultures:
Coastal cruises provide the chance to experience both nature and Norwegian maritime culture. Activities on board often include lectures about the history, customs, and marine biology of the area, giving educational insights to the journey. By stopping in coastal towns, tourists may interact with locals, see historical landmarks, and experience traditional Norwegian cuisine, including locally created specialties and freshly caught fish.

Hurtigruten's Abandonment:
For those seeking a real coastal cruise experience, Hurtigruten is a name that connotes excellence. Since 1893, Hurtigruten has operated ships around Norway's coastline, combining modern luxury with a great awareness of regional traditions and the environment. Focusing on sustainability, the cruise line shares Norway's commitment to preserving its natural beauty for future generations.

Making plans for a coastal cruise:

When planning a Norwegian coastal cruise, it is very important to consider the best time to go. Due to its moderate temperatures and lengthy daylight hours, the summer season, which lasts from June through August, is ideal for outdoor exploration. However, those who are prepared to endure the tougher months may also enjoy Norway's stunning coastline in the winter, when the Northern Lights are visible and the scenery is particularly captivating.

Finally, coastal cruises provide visitors an unrivalled opportunity to properly appreciate Norway's stunning natural surroundings, extensive maritime history, and vibrant culture. On this outdoor adventure, travellers may expect a variety of exciting encounters, including visiting fjords, passing through islands, getting close to wildlife, and mingling with locals. A Norwegian coastal cruise is more than simply a vacation; it's a transformative experience that fosters a strong connection between land and sea.

Chapter 7. Practical Tips

Language and Communication

Travelling to Norway offers a unique opportunity to see the breathtaking landscape, dynamic culture, and kind people of the Nordic nations. However, considering the linguistic diversity of the nation and the prevalence of the Norwegian language, effective communication may provide a substantial challenge for tourists. This book aims to provide travellers essential language and communication tips in order to enhance their experiences in Norway.

1. Norwegian is the official language of Norway, where the bulk of the population resides. Even though many Norwegians, especially those who live in cities and famous tourist destinations, speak English well, making an effort to acquire a few basic Norwegian phrases may greatly

enhance your interactions with locals and demonstrate that you value their culture.

2. Greetings and Basic Phrases: Learning a few fundamental greetings and phrases may make it easier for you to communicate with Norwegians. The greetings "Hei" (hello) and "God dag" (good day) are both welcome. It's essential to know how to say "Takk" (thank you) and "Unnskyld" (excuse me/sorry) in polite conversation.

3. English Proficiency: Most Norwegians, especially the younger generation, are proficient in the language. In trade and tourism, English is a widely utilised language that is taught in schools. It is still seen as polite to begin a conversation in Norwegian before switching to English.

4. Language Regions: The two recognized written varieties of the Norwegian language are Bokml and Nynorsk. Bokml is more prevalent, especially in urban regions and official papers, although Nynorsk is more frequent in other

places. While it is helpful to be aware of these distinctions, it is not required for casual conversation.

5. Cultural etiquette: When speaking with Norwegians, it's necessary to maintain a polite tone. Norwegians value their privacy and may first come off as reserved, but if a connection is struck, they are often friendly and outgoing.

6. Public Transportation: You should be aware that the majority of the signs and announcements on the buses, trams, and trains are written in both Norwegian and English if you plan to use them. Learn terms related to transportation, such as "holdeplass" (bus stop) and "billett" (ticket), to make exploration easier.

7. Dining Etiquette: Restaurants often provide English-language menus to patrons. If you want to impress your visitors, learn some culinary jargon like "Vann" (water), "Regning" (bill), and "Mat" (meal). Rounding up the bill is welcomed but not necessary.

8. Emergency Phrases: Although it's unlikely that you'll encounter an emergency, knowing how to say "Hjelp!" (assistance), "Ring politiet!" (Call the police!), and "Jeg trenger legehjelp" (I need medical assistance) may be useful in an emergency.

Travelling to Norway gives one the chance to see the country's stunning scenery and its rich culture. Effective communication is essential for making the most of your trip, whether it is in Norwegian or English. By being familiar with basic phrases and cultural etiquette, you may explore with ease, create memorable memories of your time in Norway, and form important connections with people.

Currency and Payment

Understanding the available currencies and payment options is essential as you prepare for your trip. The Norwegian Krone (NOK), which is the country's own currency, has a robust payment infrastructure. This book makes an effort to provide tourists in-depth information about currency conversion, payment choices, and suggestions to make their financial experience in Norway as easy-going as possible.

becoming familiar with the Norwegian Krone (NOK)

The legal money of Norway is the Norwegian Krone, sometimes abbreviated as NOK. Despite the fact that English is widely spoken in Norway, it is important to keep in mind that the name of the currency is derived from the Norwegian term for crown. One krone is divided into 100 re. A variety of denominations of banknotes and coins are manufactured to satisfy various transaction needs.

Currency Exchange

Before departing on your holiday to Norway, it is advisable to exchange some of your local currency into Norwegian Kroner. Currency exchange services are available at airports, banks, exchange bureaus, and a few hotels. However, it's wise to avoid doing it at the airport or a hotel since these locations can provide poorer exchange rates than banks or specialist exchange offices.

Cheap rates may also be offered through online exchange businesses, and some even deliver the money to your home. It is suggested to have a mix of cash and digital payment alternatives for flexibility.

1. Cash as Payment Options: Even though Norway is quite advanced in terms of electronic payments, having some local money on hand may be useful, especially when going to remote regions, small enterprises, or markets where cash may be the preferred mode of payment.

2. Cards, including credit and debit cards: Using credit or debit cards is quite prevalent in Norway. Visa and Mastercard are the two most used credit cards, while larger establishments may also accept American Express and Diners Club. Contactless payment is widely accepted,

which makes transactions quick and efficient. Inform your bank of your trip plans to avoid any issues using your card.

3. Mobile Payment Apps: In Norway, Vipps is a well-known mobile payment app. You may transfer money to friends, share expenses, and make payments easily thanks to them. Many businesses show QR codes for customers to scan and pay using these apps.

4. Norway has a number of automated teller machines (ATMs). The majority accept international credit cards, and they all issue Norwegian Kroner. However, pay attention to the fees your bank charges for currency conversion and withdrawals.

Advice for Successful Transactions
1. Become knowledgeable with currency rates: Keep track of the exchange rates between your home currency and the Norwegian Krone to make sure you're getting a good deal when exchanging money.

2. Choose Local Currency: When using your credit or debit card to make a purchase, choose NOK as the local currency to be used as the unit of exchange rather than your home currency. By doing this, you can prevent unjustified conversion expenses.

3. Pay Attention to Fees: Be aware of any foreign transaction fees that your bank could charge you when you use your card outside of the country. It may be worthwhile to apply for a credit card that is good for travelling and has little to no foreign transaction fees.

4. Have backup options: Even if it's customary to make payments online, having a fallback option, such as cash or a different card, might be useful in the event that anything goes wrong with the system or unanticipated events arise.

5. Be Safe: Just like you would everywhere else, use caution while using ATMs, especially in

isolated areas. Protect your PIN and be on the lookout for fraudulent card skimming.

A smooth and enjoyable trip to Norway depends on the currency and payment methods you choose. By understanding the Norwegian Krone, planning your currency conversion, and choosing the proper payment alternatives, you may enjoy Norway's natural beauty without having to worry about money. Having a solid grasp of currencies and payments will enhance your whole travel experience in this enticing Scandinavian nation, whether you're hiking through fjords, seeing historical sites, or sampling the cuisine.

Safety and Health

Norway provides a unique blend of adventure, cultural depth, and natural beauty, making a vacation there exciting. However, the preservation of visitors' health and safety must come first. This comprehensive guide aims to provide travellers a complete understanding of the security and health concerns to be mindful of when visiting Norway. This book covers a range of topics, from understanding the local environment to having emergency contacts, to ensure a safe and enjoyable holiday.

1. Getting to Know The Environment Of Norway: Fjords, mountains, and sizable woods make up some of Norway's breath-taking scenery. The breath-taking magnificence of these magnificent natural wonders is accompanied with possible risks. Travellers should research the destinations they want to visit and be informed of any potential hazards, such as avalanches, rockslides, and rapidly changing weather patterns. It's crucial to be informed about local laws and weather forecasts for a safe trip.

2. Health Precautions: Before visiting Norway, it is advisable to discuss the necessary vaccines and health precautions with a healthcare professional. A current travel insurance policy that will cover medical expenses in the event

that you become sick or harmed while travelling is something you should make sure you have. Just in case, bring a small first aid kit, any necessary prescription medications, and their prescriptions.

3. Emergency Contacts: Learn the phone numbers for Norway's emergency contacts. You may call (112) to contact the police, fire, and medical services at the same time. Contact details for the American embassy should also be provided to nationals of the United States.

4. Traffic Safety: Be aware that Norway has strict traffic regulations if you want to drive there. Seatbelts are required for all passengers, and using a phone while driving is prohibited. The roads in Norway may be tricky to drive on because of their narrow, winding bends and erratic weather.

5. Outdoor Activities: Norway offers a wide range of outdoor activities, such as hiking, skiing, and fishing. Before engaging in these

activities, be sure you are taking the necessary precautions and according to local laws. If you're hiking, let someone know your plans and anticipated return time. Skiers should be aware of the risk of avalanches and heed the advice of local authorities.

6. animal encounters: Seeing Norway's many animals might be fascinating, but it's important to maintain a safe distance. Larger animals like moose and reindeer may be deadly if approached too closely, especially during mating seasons.

7. Food and Water Safety: Norway generally enforces high standards for the hygiene of its water and food. Tap water is safe to drink around the country. Consume only seafood from trusted sources to avoid getting a foodborne illness.

8. If you're travelling alone, take extra security precautions. Share your plans with someone you can trust, and stay in contact with them. Instead of staying in distant areas, choose safe communities, especially at night.

Another cultural aspect is to respect local traditions and customs. This prevents you from unnecessarily upsetting anybody and promotes intercultural understanding. You should maintain a respectable distance from Norwegians in order to acknowledge their demand for privacy and personal space.

In conclusion, Norway offers tourists an incredible tour of its landscape and culture. Gaining the most from this event requires prioritising safety and wellness. By being informed, taking the necessary precautions, and abiding by local rules, you may travel to Norway in comfort and safety.

Chapter 8. Local Etiquette

Social Norms

Visitors should be informed of Norway's unique traditions and etiquette before travelling there since it is a stunning Scandinavian country. Norway is well known for its fjords, stunning scenery, and extensive cultural heritage. By being aware of and adhering to certain customs, visitors may more easily traverse Norwegian culture and engage with locals.

Punctuality and respect for time are highly valued in Norwegian culture. Being on time for meetings, appointments, and social events demonstrates respect for other people's time and is seen as a sign of good manners. In general, Norwegians adhere to timetables religiously, and they like it when visitors do the same.

Personal Space and Private: It's crucial to respect one another's privacy and personal space in

Norway. Since it could be considered impolite to intrude personal space, Norwegians often keep an arm's length spacing between one another during conversations. Similar to this, it is valued when intimate details are shared with some degree of care and without direct questioning.

Greetings and Interaction: When meeting someone for the first time, a firm handshake and direct eye contact are traditional. It's vital to behave properly and avoid acting out in public since Norwegians are often calm and polite. Until a closer relationship is developed, it's traditional to address them by their titles (Mr. or Mrs.) and last names.

Norwegian table manners are straightforward and modest, which is a defining characteristic of the country. It is customary to wait until the host says "vel bekomme" (bon appétit) before beginning a meal. It is customary to use the proper utensils and eat in a continental manner. Additionally, leaving a little amount of food on the plate shows that the portion size was suitable and that the meal was enjoyed.

Payment and Tipping: Gratuities are often not necessary in restaurants because service charges are frequently already included in the bill. It's usually polite to round up the check or add a little tip, however. In most places, cashless transactions are the norm, and credit and debit cards are routinely accepted.

Outdoor Behaviour: Norwegians value and protect their beautiful natural surroundings. Travellers are required to adhere to the principle of "allemannsretten," or the right to roam, which gives the general public access to the bulk of the nation's uncultivated area. Nevertheless, it's crucial to respect animals and observe "leave no trace" principles. The Norwegian concept of "friluftsliv" emphasises outside activities, therefore be prepared for unplanned trips or outdoor adventures.

Present-Giving and Social Norms

In Norwegian society, giving presents is often subdued and inexpensive. Providing a little gift, such as flowers or chocolates, is customary when being welcomed into a Norwegian person's home. Give gifts that aren't overly personal since others could find them intrusive.

Gender equality and social inclusivity: Norway is well known for its aggressive stance on these issues. It is crucial to respect individuals of all gender, sexual orientations, and origins. Your attempts to use non-discriminatory language and show an open mind will be respected by the locals.

Language and communication: Even though many Norwegians are fluent in English, trying to pick up some basic Norwegian greetings and phrases could make it easier for you to communicate with others. Locals often appreciate the gesture and may respond more amicably.

By adopting and observing Norwegian social conventions and etiquette, visitors may forge meaningful connections with locals and have a more authentic experience of Norway. Respecting these guidelines enhances the overall travel experience in this beautiful Scandinavian nation and demonstrates cultural sensitivity. They include things like being on time, respecting others' personal space, and acting appropriately outside.

Tipping Customs

Although visiting a foreign country may be exciting and enlightening, it also necessitates being acquainted with the customs and etiquette there. You'll be able to handle social situations more calmly if you are aware of the nation's tipping customs. The practice of tipping is crucial to social relationships. Norway, like many other countries, has distinct tipping traditions from those you would be used to from your own. Let's talk about Norway's customs around tipping as part of good local protocol for tourists.

1. Norway Doesn't Have a Tipping Culture: Norway is known for having a high standard of living, which is reflected in the fact that there isn't a tipping culture per se. Compared to cultures where tipping is a required part of the service industry, Norway's tipping customs are more restrained. Workers in the service sector are often adequately rewarded, which reduces their need for tips for income, and the country has a strong welfare system.

2. Norway does not need gratuities while visiting restaurants or coffee shops. However, it's customary to round the price up. Giving a generous tip of between 5 and 10% is suitable if you get exceptional service and want to show your appreciation. Locals often decide against leaving tips and pay the whole amount of the bill.

3. Hotels: Tipping is not expected but is a nice gesture if you've had excellent service. Consider leaving a little contribution on the pillow or in an envelope as a way to show the cleaning staff how much you appreciate them. Furthermore, Norway accepts gratuities for bellhops and porters.

4. Taxis: Tipping taxi drivers is not customary in Norway. However, as a token of appreciation for the service, you may round up the payment. If your fare is 175 NOK, you may simply round it up to 200 NOK. It's a quick and easy way to leave a little tip without having to calculate percentages.

5. Tipping is not necessary while participating in tours or excursions that are led. However, if you had a good day and wanted to thank your guide, you may give them a gratuity of between 50 and 100 NOK.

6. Etiquette and Cultural Considerations: Although tipping is often not a huge concern in

Norway, it is crucial to observe the local customs. The emphasis on equality and humility in Norway may make excessive gratuities inappropriate. Always be polite and thank the service staff for their assistance.

7. Service Charge and Inclusive Pricing: Look through the statement to see if any service charges have been imposed. In Norway, the total bill at restaurants and other establishments often includes a service charge. If there is a charge, gratuity is not required.

8. Cash vs. Cards: Norway's economy is mostly cashless, with most transactions occurring online. This includes gratuities. There is often a tipping option available when paying with a credit or debit card. You may tip easily online if you'd want to.

Even if tipping may not be as common in Norway as it is in some other countries, it is still crucial to understand and respect local customs. The emphasis on equality and the existence of a strong social safety net in Norway has an impact on their attitude about tipping. For very great service, it is polite to round up the payment or give a little gratuity, but extravagant tipping is not suitable here. By keeping these customs in mind, you may enjoy your trip to Norway and interact with the locals in a respectful and helpful way.

Chapter 9. Accommodation Options

Hotels and Resorts

Norway is a destination that attracts travellers from all over the world because of its vibrant culture, stunning natural beauty, and enticing landscapes. Choosing the right place to stay can significantly enhance your visit to this Nordic gem. Norway has a wide range of lodging options to accommodate a variety of preferences, ranging from luxurious resorts perched on fjords to cosy family-run inns in quaint villages.

For those seeking an affluent vacation, Norway has a large selection of luxurious hotels and resorts. Norway's fjords provide some of the most breathtaking views on earth, and many luxurious residences are situated right on the water's edge. One ancient gem in Norangsfjorden is the Hotel Union Øye, which offers opulent lodgings that provide a taste of the past together with all the modern comforts. The

Juvet Landscape Hotel in Valldal is another fantastic choice; its striking design blends in well with the surroundings.

If you would like to stay in the bustling city, Oslo offers a number of opulent options. The Thief, which is located on Tjuvholmen, has amazing views of the Oslofjord, contemporary art, and a trendy atmosphere. The Grand Hotel Oslo is a great choice for anyone who appreciates traditional elegance due to its long history and standing as a landmark in the community.

While Norway welcomes visitors staying in luxurious accommodations, it also provides an unparalleled level of comfort and care for those on a budget. For those on a limited budget who like to see the magnificence of the country, there are many affordable hotels and hostels available. Cities like Trondheim and Bergen, with their vibrant youthful cultures, are excellent places to find affordable accommodation.

For something extra special, consider scheduling a stay in a traditional Norwegian rorbu. These are former fishermen's huts that have been converted into cosy cottages by painting them a bright colour. In the Lofoten Islands, these types of accommodations are well-known for providing guests with a taste of authentic Norwegian beach life.

Adventure-seeking travellers may explore Norway's mountains and forests and find charming mountain cabins. The lodges, such as the Gjendesheim DNT Lodge in Jotunheimen National Park, provide basic but comfortable housing in the centre of the forest for hikers, skiers, and nature enthusiasts.

Norway is home to a number of top-notch wellness resorts. The Well is a health and spa facility in Oslo that offers a holistic approach to well-being with a strong emphasis on relaxation and rejuvenation. Visitors may enjoy a very unique experience in the centre of the Arctic environment at the Sorrisniva Igloo Hotel in

Alta. Visitors may experience sleeping in ice chambers and seeing the Northern Lights up close.

In Norway, there is a strong emphasis on sustainability, and there has been a discernible increase in the appeal of eco-friendly vacation spots. As mentioned before, the Juvet Landscape Hotel is an excellent example of a structure that blends in with its environment. Another notable eco-friendly choice is the off-grid Fugle Rhytta Eco-lodge, located in Oslo's woodlands. Here, you can lessen your impact on the environment while taking in the tranquillity of the woods.

In conclusion, whether you're searching for luxury, adventure, cultural immersion, or eco-friendly activities, Norway offers a huge selection of hotels and resorts to suit your demands. All travellers may choose the perfect accommodation to complement their Norwegian experience because of the country's wealth of natural beauty, charming towns, and diverse landscapes. So, while planning your trip to

Norway, consider your preferences and make the most of your stay in this enticing gem of the Nordic region.

Cabins and Cottages

For those who like to spend time in the great outdoors and get away from it all, cabins and cottages are the perfect kind of housing. These cosy retreats provide a warm and inviting space to relax while allowing you to get up close and personal with Norway's spectacular natural beauty.

One of the most iconic types of housing in Norway is the traditional Norwegian cabin, or "hytte" as it is known locally. These scattered homes around the country provide a pastoral sanctuary away from the bustle of city life. They may be found in a range of settings, such as fjords, mountains, deep forests, and coastal areas.

For those who like to experience the solitude of Norway's mountains and forests in places like Telemark, Oppland, and Hordaland, cabins are ideal. Many of these hyttes are equipped with the barest necessities, such kitchenettes, wood-burning stoves, and simple but comfortable furnishings. Renting a woodland cabin gives you access to the natural surroundings, allowing you to go hiking and skiing straight from your door.

If you want something closer to the beach, you may want to think about renting a cottage along the Norwegian coast. Coastal cottages may be found in places like the Lofoten Islands, Tromsø, and the beautiful fjord surroundings. These housing choices provide the opportunity to participate in outdoor activities like kayaking, fishing, and wildlife observation as well as to experience coastal culture. They often feature breathtaking sea views.

Lofoten Islands fishermen's cottages, or "rorbu," are a unique kind of housing. These traditional red-painted cottages, which formerly housed generations of fishermen, now dangle perilously over the water and are outfitted as cosy holiday accommodations. A stay aboard a rorbu offers a true glimpse into Norway's maritime heritage and fosters a lifetime affinity with the sea.

The offered cabins and cottages reflect Norway's rich cultural past in addition to its stunning natural surroundings. For instance, some cottages are located in charming, historic towns where you may experience a little bit of the local way of life. Some cottages are hidden close to Norway's iconic wooden stave churches, offering an opportunity to investigate these architectural treasures.

For a really unique experience, think about spending the night in a Sami tent, also called a lavvu, which is a traditional nomadic house used by the indigenous Sami people. In remote parts of Northern Norway, there are Lavvus that provide a genuine cultural immersion into the

Sami way of life, complete with reindeer herding and Arctic activities.

Norwegian cabins and cottages provide a lifestyle that is as alluring as their unique surroundings. Since many cabins and cottages let visitors self-cater, cooking your own meals with locally sourced ingredients may help you feel even more like you're in the middle of nature. Special experiences like spending time with friends over a campfire, seeing the Northern Lights dance across the Arctic sky, or just taking in the peace and quiet of a forest or fjord are made possible by these lodgings.

In conclusion, staying in Norway's cabins and cottages offers visitors an unparalleled opportunity to interact with the local nature, culture, and customs. Whether travellers are searching for a peaceful cottage by the sea, a rustic lodge in the mountains, or a historic property in a quaint hamlet, Norway has a wide range of housing alternatives to suit their needs. These retreats provide cosy accommodations together with a close-knit relationship to Norway's breathtaking natural beauty and rich cultural heritage, which make it a really amazing destination for all tourists to explore. When planning trip arrangements, consider renting a cabin or cottage so that you can fully enjoy Norway's stunning countryside and distinctive culture.

Hostels and Guesthouses

For travellers on a limited budget, finding affordable but comfortable accomodation is essential while visiting this beauty of Scandinavia. Hostels and guesthouses in Norway are fantastic options for travellers on a budget who want to see the country.

Hostels in Norway:
Hostels in Norway provide both private rooms and dorm-style lodgings, among other types of housing. Backpackers, single people, and anybody looking to meet others who have

similar hobbies all enjoy them. You may expect the following from Norwegian hostels:

1. Valuable Rates: Hostels are an excellent choice for anybody looking to save expenses while seeing Norway's sites because of their affordability. In general, hostels are significantly less costly than hotels; however, the precise price may vary depending on the kind and location of lodging.

2. The Cultural Setting: Hostels often include common areas, kitchens, and lounges where guests may socialise and swap stories. It's a great chance to network and share travel tips with people from all around the world.

3. Key Locations: Numerous hostels are conveniently located in the heart of cities or close to well-known tourist attractions. This facilitates guests' access to dining establishments, tourism destinations, and public transportation.

4. Required Minimum Facilities: While they are budget-friendly housing alternatives, hostels nevertheless provide conventional amenities like free WiFi, clean bathrooms, and sometimes even breakfast. Some hostels go above and beyond by organising events and providing laundry facilities for their guests.

5. Variety of Room Types: Hostels often provide a variety of lodging alternatives, including mixed and female-only dorms, in addition to private rooms. It is up to the visitors to choose the level of privacy that best suits their need and budget.

Guesthouses in Norway:
Guesthouses are cosier and more intimate than hostels when it comes to housing. They are often small, family-run companies that provide guests a unique and personal experience. The following is what to expect from guesthouses in Norway:

1. Warm Salutations: Guesthouses are well known for providing personalised and friendly

services. It is typical for owners to have a strong desire to ensure that their guests have a comfortable and joyful stay.

2. Recreation Areas: Many guesthouses are found in picturesque settings, such as fjords, mountains, and rural areas. Those who stay in guesthouses may take full use of Norway's beautiful surroundings.

3. Local Cuisine: There are guesthouses that provide their guests traditional Norwegian cuisine. You get to try local food, which can turn out to be the highlight of your trip.

4. Comfortable Ambience: Guesthouses tend to have cosier, more relaxed ambiances since they often have fewer rooms available. This is perfect for those searching for a quiet retreat after a day of touring.

5. Experiences with Culture: Owners of guesthouses may educate guests about local

traditions and culture, improving their understanding of Norwegian culture.

Hostels and guesthouses in Norway provide visitors the opportunity to explore the country's stunning fjords, thrilling Northern Lights, vibrant city life in Oslo, Bergen, and Trondheim, and the unique Sami culture up north.

Whether you choose a hostel for the affordable and social atmosphere or a guesthouse for the intimate experience and local flavour, both options offer unique opportunities to completely immerse yourself in the beauty of Norway. So whether you're a backpacker or a tourist seeking a more personalised experience, Norway's hostels and guesthouses have something special to offer throughout your travels around this Nordic beauty.

Chapter 10. Itinerary Ideas

One Week in Norway

A week in Norway is an enticing opportunity to completely immerse oneself in the breathtaking landscape and lively culture of this hidden gem of Scandinavia. A week might not be enough to explore all that Norway has to offer, from the vibrant cities to the stunning fjords and unique cultural experiences. Here is a suggested schedule for individuals who wish to make the most of their seven days in Norway:

Day 1: Arrival in Oslo
Take a plane to Oslo, the largest and capital city of Norway, to start your journey. Spend the first day exploring this energetic city. Highlights include the magnificent Oslo Opera House, Vigeland Park with its iconic sculptures, and the Royal Palace. Explore Karl Johans Gate, Oslo's main street, and indulge in delicious Norwegian cuisine at local restaurants.

Day 2 : Touring Oslo
On the second day, go further exploring across Oslo. Discover the rich history of Norway by taking a boat journey to the Bygdøy Peninsula and seeing the Fram Museum and the Kon-Tiki Museum. Additionally, you may go to the Viking Ship Museum. To end the day, take a leisurely walk along the beach at Aker Brygge.

Day 3: Bergen and the Fjords
Enjoy a charming train trip from Bergen to Oslo. The real hike offers amazing vistas as it winds over mountains and along fjord rims. Explore Bergen's Bryggen Wharf, a UNESCO World Heritage site. Travel to Mount Fløyen on the Fløibanen Funicular for breathtaking views of the city and neighbouring fjords.

Day 4 : Explore the Fjords
Take a day trip that leaves from Bergen and go further into the fjords. The Naerøyfjord is a must-see fjord on the UNESCO list. Take a boat

or bus trip to see the spectacular, little canal's surrounding high cliffs. Return to Bergen and unwind at one of the many seafood restaurants in the area for the evening.

Day 5: Trondheim's Historic Charm
Visit the historically and culturally rich city of Trondheim. See the magnificent Gothic Nidaros Cathedral by taking a stroll along the Nidelva River. Admire the city's unique blend of modern and historical features.

Day 6 : Earthing the Lofoten Islands
After taking a plane to Bodø, take a ferry to reach the Lofoten Islands. Popular attractions on this remote island include its wild landscapes, fishing villages, and outdoor activities like hiking and kayaking. As you spend the day discovering this beautiful natural area, savour the flavour of freshly caught fish.

Day 7: Heading Back to Oslo
Return to Oslo on your last day of travel across Norway. Visit the Munch Museum to see the

well-known Norwegian artist Edvard Munch. Included in the display is "The Scream." In the evening, stroll slowly along the Oslofjord and enjoy the serene surroundings and stunning landscape.

Although this one-week itinerary highlights some of Norway's natural beauty and cultural riches, it's vital to remember that there are still many more treasures to be found in this vast country. While it is up to the individual tourist to tailor their itinerary to suit their interests, this guide offers a well-rounded experience that combines city life, stunning landscape, and cultural immersion. Norway is a destination worth visiting, even for a week, due to its breathtaking landscapes and kind, welcoming populace.

Two Weeks in Norway

For those who like to really immerse themselves in the minute aspects of this magnificent nation in Scandinavia, a two-week tour throughout Norway is an absolute dream come true. You may enjoy a lengthier, more thorough trip to Norway with a two-week stay, which includes stunning fjords, Arctic experiences, bustling cities, and the magical Northern Lights. Those who are willing to spend two weeks seeing the country may find the following comprehensive vacation itinerary:

First Week: Southern Norway Tour

Day 1: Arrival in Oslo

To start your adventure, take an aeroplane to Oslo, the capital of Norway. On your first day, take an easy walk along the Aker Brygge waterfront neighbourhood, pay a visit to the Viking Ship Museum, and discover the cultural and historical gems of the city.

Day 2: Oslo's Cultural Heritage

Examine Oslo's cultural landscape in more depth. Visit the Munch Museum, which is home to well-known works such as "The Scream."

Explore the Bygdøy Peninsula, which is home to stunning beaches and aquariums.

Day 3 : Trondheim

Visit the mediaeval city of Trondheim, which is well-known for its charming old town and stunning Nidaros Cathedral. Enjoy the unique blend of old and new components of the city by taking a walk along the Nidelva River.

Day 4: Bergen and the Fjords

Take the stunning train from Trondheim to Bergen. Bergen is well-known for two things: the Fløibanen Funicular, which offers stunning views of the city and fjord, and Bryggen Wharf, a UNESCO World Heritage site.

Day 5: Fjord Exploration

Spend a day exploring the fjords to get a better look. Discover the UNESCO-listed Naerøyfjord, a small yet breathtaking river encircled by towering cliffs. This evening, return to Bergen for a seafood supper.

Day 6: Stavanger and Preikestolen

To start your trip to the well-known Preikestolen (Pulpit Rock), go to Stavanger. Visit this well-known cliff for a day excursion to see the magnificent views of the Lysefjord.

Day 7 : Lofoten Islands

From Bodø, go to the Lofoten Islands via ferry. These remote islands provide breathtaking landscapes, fishing villages, and a range of outdoor activities including hiking and kayaking.

Week 2: Northern Norway and the Arctic

Day 8: Tromsø's Arctic Gateway

Fly to Tromsø, the capital of Arctic Norway. Explore the city and enjoy its thriving cultural scene and stunning Arctic Cathedral.

Days 9–10: Northern Lights and Arctic Adventures

Spend a few days exploring the Arctic's wilderness. Try your hand at dog sledding, snowmobiling, and chasing the Northern Lights.

Day 11: Alta and the Northern Lights Cathedral

Proceed to Alta, the location of the Northern Lights Cathedral. To learn more about prehistoric rock carvings, visit the Alta Museum.

Day 12: Kirkenes and the Russian Border

Take a look at Kirkenes, a town on the Russian border. Benefit from a king crab safari or an exclusive stay at a snow hotel.

Day 13: Returning to Oslo

Fly back to Oslo on your last full day in Norway. Take some time to revisit some of your favourite locations or discover new attractions that you missed on your first visit.

Day 14: Final Departure

With a heart full of amazing experiences and priceless memories, bid Norway farewell.

This two-week itinerary gives you a thorough introduction to Norway, including everything from the wonders of the northern Arctic to the southern cultural hubs. Remember that you may tailor your vacation to fit your interests and that Norway provides a wide variety of landscapes and cultures. This amazing voyage will reveal the beauty and charm of Norway, whether you are attracted to its vibrant towns, breathtaking fjords, or both.

Northern Lights Adventure

Seeing the Northern Lights in Norway is a dream come true for a lot of travellers. Known by a variety of names, the Aurora Borealis is a spectacular natural phenomenon that paints the Arctic sky in vivid colours, creating an enchanting spectacle that astounds spectators. Some of the best opportunities to see this fascinating spectacle are in the northern regions of Norway, such as Tromsø and Alta. All the details you need to plan a vacation to Norway to see the Northern Lights are provided here.

1. Location and Time:

In Norway, late September to early April is the greatest time to observe the Northern Lights, with late September to early March being the finest viewing window. Tromsø, Alta, and Kirkenes, and other locations in the extreme north, are excellent places to be since they are closer to the Arctic Circle and have less light pollution. Tromsø, also referred to as the "Gateway to the Arctic," is particularly well-liked for its Northern Lights excursions.

2. Experiences and Tours with Guides:

To increase your chances of witnessing the Northern Lights, choose a guided tour. Expert tour guides can direct you to the finest viewing spots since they are knowledgeable about the local weather and aurora forecasts. Warm clothing, transportation, and hot refreshments are often provided for these trips to guarantee your comfort during the event.

3. Winter Seasonal Events:

When it comes to trips to see the northern lights, Norway has more to offer than just aurora hunting. You may combine your hunt for the lights with a variety of seasonal activities. Snowmobiling, dog sledding, and cross-country skiing are popular pursuits that allow you to explore the Arctic landscape during the day and search for lights at night.

4. Arctic Accommodations:

For a really true Northern Lights experience, stay in unique accommodations like glass igloos or ice lodges. These structures provide cosy lodging in addition to unobstructed views of the night sky. Imagine yourself lounging on a warm bed as the Northern Lights twinkle above!

5. Put on Cosy Clothing

Bring warm clothing and layers of clothing since the Arctic is quite cold. To guarantee your comfort while seeing the Northern Lights, you must dress appropriately for the weather.

Insulated boots, hats, and thermal clothing are examples of such items.

6. Patience Is the Key:
It's not always possible to observe the Northern Lights since they are a naturally occurring phenomenon that relies on solar activity and atmospheric conditions. You may have to be patient and stay a few nights to view the lights at their best.

7. Camera Configuration:
If you're an amateur photographer wanting to capture the Northern Lights, make sure you pack a tripod and turn your camera to manual. It frequently takes a long exposure to capture its ethereal beauty.

8. Cultural Experiences:
While you wait for the lights to turn on, totally immerse yourself in the community. Eat Arctic specialties like king crab and discover the history and culture of the region by visiting

museums. You may also learn about the Sami people who live there.

9. Honor and Nature Preservation:
Remember to be aware of and respectful of the local wildlife and environment. When engaging with animals, follow moral guidelines and don't leave any trash behind.

It's a once-in-a-lifetime opportunity to go to Northern Lights viewing in Norway. The magical kaleidoscope of colours in the Arctic sky is an incredible sight that will never get old. Consider every detail of your journey, from clothing to guided tours to the ideal time to visit Norway's most northern areas, in order to maximise your chances of seeing this celestial event. After your journey, you'll have memories of a unique natural gem that not many people get to view.

Chapter 11. Useful Phrases

Basic Norwegian Phrases for Travelers

Learning a few simple Norwegian words before visiting Norway is usually a smart idea. Though English is widely spoken in Norway, you might still have a better travel experience and more pleasurable interactions if you try to learn their language. Throughout your journey, you'll find the following important Norwegian terms useful:

Salutations - Hi- Hei, which is pronounced "hay".

Good day– Go morgen, which is pronounced "go mor-gen"

Good Evening / afternoon. - Go ettermiddag/kveld, which is pronounced as "go ed-er-mi-dag/kveld".

So long "Ha det" is pronounced as "ha deh".

Empathising Words: - Thanks for the welcome. - Vær så god, which is pronounced "ver saw goh".

Let me apologise - Pronounce Unnskyld as "oon-skyld"

Emergency Words or Expressions - Help - Hjelp (pronounced "yelp").

A physician is required - Jeg trenger en lege (pronounced "yay treng-er en lay-geh").

Keep in mind that even if you just speak a few simple words, Norwegians value your attempt to communicate in their language. In addition to improving your ability to navigate and communicate, knowing these words will enhance the cultural richness and enjoyment of your travels. When travelling across Norway's breathtaking scenery and energetic towns, keeping a phrasebook or translation software close at hand may also be very helpful.

My Experience

As the plane descended through a quilted layer of clouds, my heart raced with anticipation. I had always wanted to go to Norway, a place renowned for its stunning fjords, thriving cities, and pristine natural beauty. When the wheels landed in Norway, I hardly believed what I was seeing.

On my first morning in Oslo, a soft, ethereal light appeared to have coated the city with a warm, golden tinge. Both locals and tourists were moving about their everyday lives on the streets, which were busy with bustle. The architectural fusion of modern and ancient buildings demonstrated the city's rich history and forward-thinking mindset.

Visitors were drawn to Vigeland Park by the promise of sculptured wonders. As I walked down the cobblestone walkways, I was met with amazing sculptures that seemed to come to life. Gustav Vigeland's artwork preserved emotions and stories in stone and created a deep sense of kinship with the human condition.

In order to get to Bergen, a little beach town encircled by formidable mountains, I took a train and left the city behind. One of the world's most spectacular train excursions, the Flam Railway took me through a landscape of snow-capped peaks, flowing waterfalls, and verdant valleys. Every time the rails swerved and twisted, a new perspective would appear, leaving me gasping for air and reaching for my camera.

The town's stunning wooden residences struck me as a striking reminder of its maritime heritage when I first arrived in Bergen. The ancient Bryggen Wharf, a UNESCO World Heritage Site, transported me to a period of lively trade and Hanseatic merchants. At the fish market, I ate local delicacies while inhaling the salty sea air and tasting fresh seafood.

But the fjords were where my trip to Norway really came to life. By boat, we explored the

Naeroyfjord and the Aurlandsfjord, where we were awestruck by the beauty of nature. Towering rocks welcomed the lovely waters as waterfalls tumbled down the granite faces like shimmering threads. As the boat glided by mirror-like reflections, a lovely peace enveloped me, and I felt a strong connection to the untamed nature.

In Troms, the location of the northern lights and the midnight sun, I had the opportunity to feel the magic of the Arctic. The sun's brilliant light, which would not set, illuminated the countryside in shades of gold and pink. The sky was a mix of green and blue at night, when the elusive auroras created their celestial canvases.

The culmination of my excursion was a hike to Preikestolen, also referred to as the Pulpit Rock. After meandering through the forests and up the difficult terrain, the journey ended at a stunning cliff that provided a breathtaking view of the Lysefjord. As I stood on the edge of the globe with the wind tickling my hair, I experienced a heady combination of excitement and humility. The view served as an unfathomably beautiful reward and a tribute to both my own tenacity and the beauty of the world.

As I reluctantly got on the plane to go back home, I brought memories with me that would be etched in my heart for a very long time. Norway's beauty, its kind people, and its flawless marriage of tradition and contemporary had left a lasting impression on my spirit. When I first came upon this beauty, it ignited my wanderlust and made me desire to explore more of this amazing world. And as I saw the Norwegian coastline go into the distance, I understood that this was only the beginning of my adventures.

Chapter 12. Additional Resources

Websites and Apps

Websites and apps have revolutionised traveller planning, navigation, and enhancement for travel to foreign countries, including Norway. Whether you're searching for travel tips, local recommendations, information on places to see, or even language translation, these online tools might be of great assistance. The websites and apps in the following list are intended for tourists travelling to Norway:

Links:

1.Go to www.visitnorway.com to learn more about Norway: This official Innovation Norway website has a wealth of information on trip places, activities, and advice. It's a great place to start when planning your trip.

2. The Norwegian Institute of Meteorology (yr.no): Yr provides reliable national weather forecasts despite Norway's unpredictable weather. For planning outdoor activities and creating thoughtful packing lists, it's an essential tool.

3. NSF (nsb.no): The Norwegian State Railways (NSB) website allows you to buy tickets, see route details, and view train schedules. It comes in very handy while traversing Norway by rail.

4. Flytoget (flytoget.no): If you're flying, you may buy tickets for the 19-minute ride on the airport express train from Oslo Airport to the city centre on the Flytoget website.

5. Fjord Tours (www.fjordtours.com): Fjord Tours is a great resource for planning fjord cruises and other amazing trips in Norway. To explore the country's natural splendour, you may make travel plans, peruse itineraries, and check into other options.

6. ruter (ruter.no): If you're planning to use public transportation, such buses, trams, or ferries, Ruter's website is a fantastic place to start.

7. Couchsurfing.com/Cooper Surfing : If you're on a limited budget, Couchsurfing links you with locals who provide free accomodation and a special chance for cultural contact.

[Apps]

1. Go to Norway on iOS and Android: The official Visit Norway app has details on attractions, activities, and travel tips. It is a helpful tool for trip planning.

2. Norwegian (Android/iOS) : Although you may encounter linguistic obstacles, the Norwegian app facilitates the acquisition of essential vocabulary and improves your ability to interact with locals.

3. iOS/Android Google Translate: This versatile tool makes it easier to converse in the native language by facilitating text and voice translation.

4. iOS/Android Maps.me: You may obtain precise offline maps of Norway from Maps.me. It is absolutely important for travelling to remote areas without cell service.

5. You can buy train and bus tickets, check schedules, and get journey updates with the easy-to-use Vy app. It is NSB's iOS/Android counterpart.

6. Check out OSLO (iOS/Android): The VisitOSLO app provides details on events, local activities, and cuisine options when visiting the country's capital.

7. SAS (Android/iOS): With their app, Scandinavian Airlines (SAS) offers flight information, mobile boarding cards, and other helpful features.

8. iOS/Android/YR : The Norwegian Meteorological Institute's mobile app, YR, is an addition to their website that provides real-time weather forecasts.

9. Android/iOS TIDE: TIDE offers real-time information for trams, buses, and ferries in Oslo and the surrounding region.

10. Uber on iOS/Android : Uber is helpful for getting about Bergen and Oslo, however it's limited to certain cities.

These tools and apps provide assistance with anything from preparing to translating between languages, getting about, and finding current information. They are meant to make your journey to Norway easier, more efficient, and more enjoyable. You can make the most of your vacation to this stunning Scandinavian country by adopting these contemporary technologies, whether you're exploring the vibrant capital, picturesque fjords, or the wonders of the northern Arctic.

THANK YOU FOR READING......

Made in United States
Troutdale, OR
01/04/2024

16633683R00086